CW01494448

MAKE TWITTER WORK FOR YOUR BUSINESS

The complete guide
to marketing your business,
generating leads, finding
new customers and building
your brand on Twitter.

Alex Stearn

Copyright © 2016 Alex Stearn
AMS Media and Publishing Ltd
All rights reserved

© 2014 by Alex Stearn
AMS Media and Publishing Ltd
Exterior cover , internal design and contents
© Alex Stearn
All rights reserved.
The rights to reproduce the work are reserved to the copyright holder.

No part of this publication may be reproduced, stored in a retrieval system,
distributed, or transmitted in any form or by any means, electronic or mechanical,
photocopying, recording, scanning or otherwise without the prior written permission
of the publisher, except in the case of brief quotations embodied in critical reviews
and certain other non commercial uses permitted by copyright law. For permission
requests, write to the publisher, Alexandra Stearn.

All the business names, product names and brand names used in this book are
trademarks, trade names or registered trademarks of their respective owners and I am
not associated with any product, business entity or company. The views, opinions
and strategies in this book are purely those of the author.

Limit of Liability / Disclaimer of Warranty. While the publisher and author have used
their best efforts in preparing this book, they make no representations or warranties
with the respect to the accuracy or completeness of the contents of this book
specifically disclaim any implied warranties of merchantability or fitness for a
particular purpose. No warranty maybe created or extended by sales representatives
or written sales materials. The advice and strategies contained herein may not be
suitable for your situation. You should consult with a professional where appropriate.
Neither the publisher or the author shall be liable for any loss of profit or any
commercial damages, including but not limited to special, incidental, consequential,
or other damages.

Although the author and publisher have made every effort to ensure that the
information in this book was correct at press time, the author and publisher do not
assume and hereby disclaim any liability to any party for any loss, damage, or
disruption caused by errors or omissions, whether such errors or omissions result
from negligence, accident, or any other cause. While every effort is made to ensure
that all the information in this book is accurate and up to date, we accept no
responsibility for keeping the information up to date or any liability for any failure to
do so.

Copyright © 2016 Alex Stearn

AMS Media and Publishing Ltd

All rights reserved.

This book is dedicated
to Sonia, Tony and Ollie.

Any Questions?

Thank you for your recent purchase of 'Make Twitter Work for your Business' I really hope you enjoy the book and your business will benefit greatly.

If you have any questions about the book or about social media marketing in general, please do not hesitate to contact me by email at **alex@alexstearn.com** or on Facebook or Twitter and I will do my best to reply as soon as possible. I also offer regular updates, ebooks and social media tips in my newsletter at www.alexstearn.com and a group on Facebook which is all about supporting each other in our social media efforts and networking. Would love you to join us at this link http://bit.ly/yourgroup

Looking forward to seeing you in the group 😊

Table of Contents

WHY THIS BOOK?

SO YOU WANT to launch a Twitter marketing campaign for your business or maybe you've already done so and you're just not achieving the results you expected. Perhaps that's because you've found it difficult to build a sizeable following or your audience is simply not converting into paying customers.

Every day hundreds of businesses are setting out on their social media journey excited about the opportunities and possibilities that this relatively new type of marketing may be able to offer their business. Some are getting it right, reaping huge rewards, and managing to leverage the enormous power of the Internet through social media, but the majority are struggling to make it work at all. Those who are struggling often don't really understand exactly how social media works and launch into a campaign without any plan or strategy or without even knowing exactly what they are looking to achieve. They perhaps create a Twitter profile and ask their web developer to add a 'like' or 'follow' button to their website, invite their friends and customers to join their page, and then start posting updates. After a while they realize that whatever they are doing is having little or no positive effect on their sales and they are left with the same questions:

- How do I leverage the almighty power of the Internet and Twitter to make money for my business?
- How do I find the people who are interested in my products?
- How do I draw these people away from Twitter and onto my website or blog?
- And the ultimate question, how do I convert all these people into paying customers and actually profit from Twitter marketing?

These businesses either continue to go round in circles waiting for a miracle to happen, give up altogether, or continue to believe that there is a way they can make social media work for their business and start looking for a solution to solve their problem.

This is exactly what I did and this is where my social media journey began. I started to look for a solution but kept coming up with the same brick walls, the same fluffy vague information about engagement, and lots of very expensive courses. I read books and blogs but they never really seemed to solve my problem and get to the heart of the matter.

I then decided to make it my mission to demystify the hype surrounding social media marketing and discover everything I possibly could about how to make all the major social media platforms work for any business. I studied literally hundreds of campaigns to see what was working and what wasn't and completely immersed myself in social media marketing until all my questions were answered. My aim was to discover how to utilize the almighty power of Twitter to help any business achieve their marketing goals. I made it my mission to leave no stone unturned in terms of a marketing opportunity which could help any business generate leads and ultimately increase their sales.

After 18 months of immersing myself in this subject, I am now delighted to hand this information over to you. My goal is to help you save your time and your resources and provide you with a highly effective system to make Twitterwork for your business. In this book I am going to share with you everything you need to know to take your business to the next level and leverage the power of Twitterso you can achieve the highest profits, the best customers, the best ambassadors for your business, and make money 24/7.

This book is perfect for anyone who is seriously committed to growing their business and achieving incredible results. Whether you are just starting out or already up and running and uncertain how to make Twitter work for your business then this book is to going to teach you exactly how to do just that. You will have absolutely everything you need to learn, prepare, plan, and implement a campaign which is going to help you generate leads and find new customers.

The fact is, Twitter, and social media as a whole, is a game changer, a dream come true for any business and has completely revolutionized the way business is being done today. However, it is still just a marketing tool and while on the face of it seems free, if not used correctly and effectively, it is simply just a waste of your time and resources.

In this book you will not only learn the skills and strategies of Twitter marketing but also everything you need to know about how social media works in marketing and how to plan, prepare, and execute your campaign including:

> What social media marketing is, why it is so good, why it is absolutely essential for any business today, and why so many businesses are getting it wrong
>
> The psychology behind why people make buying decisions and how you can use this knowledge to succeed in your Twitter campaign and other social media campaigns as well
>
> The importance of defining your business, your brand, and your target audience and how to do this
>
> How to set clear goals and objectives for your social media campaign
>
> How to prepare your website or blog for success, capture leads, and build a highly targeted list of subscribers
>
> How to plan, create, maintain, and manage your Twitter campaign
>
> Detailed information about how to set up your business profile on Twitter
>
> The strategies you need to implement to attract the best

prospects and build and maintain a targeted following on Twitter and build lasting relationships

The importance of content and how to easily find ideas to create content for your page

How to convert your followers into leads, paying customers, and ambassadors and brand advocates of your business

How to constantly measure and monitor your campaign so you can steer your campaign to achieve your goals

A great deal of love and joy has gone into writing this book. Love of the subject itself and joy at the opportunity to share with you the information and knowledge within. I have devoted 18 months to researching and writing this book, along with the others in the series, in order to uncover the truth about social media. I truly hope you will be inspired and that your business will thrive and flourish by implementing the suggested strategies.

As mentioned above there are books available on Kindle and in paperback for each of the major social media platforms including Facebook, Instagram, Twitter , LinkedIn, Google + YouTube, Pinterest and Tumblr. The big book, 'Make Social Media Work for your Business'includes all 8 books. If you are planning on buying more than a few books then I would suggest purchasing this book rather than each individual book. The big book 'Make Social Media Work for your Business' is available from $9.99 at this Link.

Even within the time it has taken to write this book, certain things have changed in the social media world and so some sections have been updated to reflect those changes. The world of social media is dynamic and therefore it is my commitment to keep updating this book as those changes occur. If you wish to keep up-to-date with latest social media updates, tips, and changes, please subscribe to my newsletter at www.alexstearn.com

The Social Media Master Plan
& Workbook
Now FREE to download

The Social Media Planner and Workbook compliments this book and all the books in the series 'Make Social Media Work for your Business'. Once you have read the book I highly recommend that you complete this short workbook. It's designed to take you step by step through what you need to do to find your ideal customers, build your audience on social media and actually succeed to selling your products and services. It is not a substitute for reading the book but will help you apply your knowledge to your particular product or service.

You can download your **FREE** Ebook here:

www.bit.ly/winsocial

CHAPTER ONE

THE IMPORTANCE OF UNDERSTANDING SOCIAL MEDIA MARKETING

BEFORE LAUNCHING INTO your Twitter marketing campaign, and so that you are absolutely committed when you do start, you will need to be convinced that social media marketing does actually work for businesses and that you are going to be able to make it work for yours. In this chapter, you will learn why social media marketing has gained so much attention, why so many brands are using it, and why it is so different from other forms of marketing. The aim here is to help you truly appreciate the power and importance of this relatively new method of marketing. Once you are totally convinced that the time you will be investing will be truly worthwhile, you will be ready to launch into your Twitter marketing campaign with strength, confidence, and conviction.

So what is social media exactly? Social media is the place where people connect with other people using the technology we have today. It's where people engage, share, cooperate, interact, learn, enjoy, and build relationships. The number of ways in which we connect with each other has grown massively in recent years from telephone, mobiles, email, text, video, newspaper, or radio to what we have today, the social media networks.

As humans, the majority of us want to belong, be accepted, loved, respected, and heard. We are social animals and social media has provided us with new tools which allow us to be more social, even if our lives are more hectic and we are living a long way from our friends and family. It's now not unusual for family and friends to be located at opposite sides of the country or even in a different country. Our lives have become far busier and more transient than ever, and yet we still crave the same social connections as we did 100 years ago when we would probably have been living in the same village or town as our family and friends.

The impact that social media is having on our lives and on businesses is massive. Social media has completely changed the way we communicate and the way we do everything. It has made connecting with people and building relationships so much easier. Now, staying in contact with someone we may only have met once is straightforward. We can find old friends we went to school or college with, and the opportunities for making new contacts are limitless. Social media has given us the ability to quickly and easily share ideas, experiences, and information on anything we like, and we can find out about anyone, any business, or anything. With the massive growth in smartphone ownership, most people can now access the internet instantly. We are living in a virtual world and we can literally connect to anyone, from anywhere, at anytime.

Understanding the reasons why people love social media so much will help give you a really good idea about how, as a business, you need to engage so you can connect,grow and maintain that your audience. Most people are on social media to be social, to connect with other family and friends, and to have fun. However, here are a few more reasons why so many use and love social media:

To be part of a community or common interest group
To express their feelings and have a voice
To reconnect with old college or school friends
To find out where their friends are
To tell their friends where they are
To announce a piece of news
To find out if a product or service is good

To connect with thought leaders

To make business contacts

To follow brands

To keep up-to-date with current affairs, football scores etc

To connect with famous people

To find inspiration and motivation

To learn by reading blogs, watching videos, and listening to podcasts

To help other people

To launch a business

To advertise and grow a business

To make new friends

To make new contacts

To connect with others in different countries

To make a difference

To be entertained

To communicate quickly and save time

To support important causes or people

To find a job

The power and enormity of social media

Everyone is doing Social! Okay, so not everyone is, but the majority of people are! Wherever you go you will see somebody with their heads down looking at some device, and you can bet your bottom dollar that they are accessing some social site, whether it's, Twitter, Facebook, Instagram, LinkedIn, YouTube, Google+, Pinterest, or Snapchat.

The growth in social media is huge, and it's no wonder that it is being called 'The Social Media Revolution.' Without going into too much statistical information, it's safe to say that your customer is probably using at least one social network, either for personal or business use, and they very likely accessing multiple sites.

All the social media platforms are growing at incredible speeds. You only have to type 'Social media statistics' into Google and you will blown away by figures in the millions and billions. Facebook now has over one billion users and 95% of those users access it at least once a day and some more than five times, a day More than one billion unique users visit YouTube per month, and Twitter has 215 monthly active users. The most popular websites are social. The world loves being on social.

WHAT IS SOCIAL MEDIA MARKETING

Not long ago promoting a business could feel very much like being alone on a desert island. You could have a great idea but unless you had vast sums of money for television, magazine, or direct mail advertising then, frustratingly, your idea was very likely to remain a secret. Today it is totally different and social media has given businesses endless opportunities to reach their target audience, connect with new prospects, and enter new markets. The playing field has been leveled out, and now anyone with the right knowledge has more chance than ever of making their business a success.

Social media marketing is a relatively new form of marketing and refers to the processes, strategies, and tactics used by businesses on social networking sites and blogs to gain attention and ultimately increase their revenue. Businesses and large brands are now using the fact that people love to engage and connect with other people with the other important fact that they are very likely to find their target audience on social media so that they can do the following:

- Find, reach, and connect with potential customers
- Drive traffic to a website or blog
- Stay connected and communicate with existing customers. It is a well-known fact that existing customers are far more likely to purchase and also pay more for a product than someone who has not bought before.
- To build trust, interest, and loyalty by interacting with your followers (potential customers) so that ultimately they will purchase your product, continue to purchase your product, and

hopefully recommend your product to their friends

- To produce content that users will share with their social network or recommend to their friends. Social media marketing strongly centers around the creation of content for a particular audience with the intention that it can be shared, 'liked', and commented on by the user. When this happens, the content is being passed to other users by word-of-mouth, the most powerful form of advertising.
- To listen and find out what your customers want

THE BIG LINK, THE PSYCHOLOGY BEHIND BUYING BEHAVIOUR

Not only have successful marketeers recognized that people want to engage with people, they have also tapped into the psychology behind why people make buying decisions and incorporated this into their social media campaigns.

As a business you will need to understand a great deal about your customers in order to market your products successfully to your target audience. Understanding how and why people make the final purchase decision will go a long way to help you discern how to make social media marketing actually work for your business. There seem to be a number of common factors that influence consumers when they are making their buying decision. Leveraging and using this knowledge with your Twitter campaign will be incredibly powerful and a recipe for success.

The Like factor

This is a Biggie. When we look at the findings and the psychology behind buying decisions it often comes down to simply being likeable. Consumers are far more likely buy a product from someone they like, respect or trust. Word of mouth advertising has always proven to be the most powerful form of advertising and now Twitter has taken this to another level and managed to harness this online with the tweet and 'retweet'. Having your business name or brand reach hundreds or even thousands of people is now possible and someone only has to interact with your business on social media and you can almost guarantee that someone else will see it. The truth is people do business with people they like and are more likely to spread the word to their network about deals and special offers from people they like, trust and respect.

Social proof

When a consumer finds themselves at a point of indecision they will look for social proof and seek advice and corroboration from others. They are far more likely to buy if they see that their friends or a similar group of people have bought or used product. People generally look to others for advice or look to see what others are buying to get over their personal insecurity when making a buying decision. This is why you see so many women shopping in pairs, the opinion of a friend about an item can often be the deciding factor when making the decision to buy or not.

The reason this is so powerful with social media marketing is simply because seeing a large number of people 'liking' a product or service can be enough to persuade someone to make a buying decision, to read something or follow a business. The truth is that people trust the opinion of others more than they trust advertising and in order to make social media marketing work then businesses need to leverage this fact.

Authority and reviews

Even before the Internet was introduced, people were keen to find reviews about products they were interested in buying, particularly if they were planning to make a major purchase. They would either buy a special magazine or seek information from an authoritative figure on a TV advertisement. Today, however, shoppers are far more savvy. They can smell an ad a mile off and they will go out of their way to find honest reviews about something they may want to buy. They are also spoiled for choice, not only with the number of products available to them but the fact that they can find a review about literally anything just by a simple search on the Internet. People always have and always will want as much evidence as possible that they are making the right buying decision. Any business who wants to succeed today needs to embrace this fact and try and gain as many reviews for their products and services as possible. Reviews could be in the form of customer blog articles, reviews on your website, on social media sites, or articles in newspapers and magazines. Displaying articles, client testimonials, or the logos of magazines that you have been featured in on your website will also go a long way to building authority and gaining the trust of your prospects.

Scarcity or exclusivity

Scarcity or exclusivity can play a big part in people's buying decisions, and Twitter is a perfect place to communicate and use this factor to sell your products. If a product is scarce or less available, the consumer will often perceive that this product has greater value. As it becomes less available, the consumer fears that they may lose out on a great deal or a one-time offer. Giving your prospects a deadline or a specific time to purchase something or redeem an offer is an incredibly powerful way of focusing their mind on making a decision. When they know they need to make that decision by a certain time or they may lose out on a one-time deal, they are far more likely to make that decision. Another very effective way of using this factor is by simply suggesting to your prospects that by signing up for your email opt-in, they will be the first to hear about your new products or your exclusive offers.

Loyalty

Consumers do not like taking risks and often prefer to repeat their past purchasing behavior by buying from a brand they have bought from before. The majority of shoppers are brand loyal and social media is another way of nurturing this type of behavior by building up even deeper relationships with your customers through constant contact and updates.

Reciprocation

Reciprocation is a very powerful factor to take into consideration if you are looking to succeed on Twitter. As humans, the majority of us have a natural desire to repay favors and with Twitter you can really put this into practice. By 'liking', sharing, or commenting on other people's content, you will attract their attention.. More often than not, they will return the favor by 'liking', commenting, and sharing your content. Also, if you are sharing great content on your network or offering good, valuable, and free advice, you are very likely to earn a great deal of respect. This will often result in a good payback of some sort later.

WHY IS SOCIAL MEDIA MARKETING SO GOOD FOR YOUR BUSINESS?

We know that an enormous number of people are accessing the social networks to connect with each other and now we need to understand why this type of marketing is so different from other forms of marketing and why it is so important for your business. The main reason is that social media marketing is fundamentally more effective. Consumers today are smart, they are tired and suspicious of traditional forms of advertising, more often than not they will fast forward a TV commercial, switch channel or skip a printed page with an advertisement on it. Today's consumers want to hear that a product has been tried and tested, they want to see a product being demonstrated and they often need a recommendation from a trusted source to make a purchase, most probably a friend. Here are some reasons why social media marketing is more effective than other more traditional marketing methods:

Social media offers you the opportunity to find the right target audience

Never before has it been so easy to find and access your target audience. With the information that Twitter and most of the social networks hold about their users you can now target and find the very people who are more likely to buy your products or services.

Social media allows you to have a direct contact with your customer

Literally you have the opportunity to communicate directly and stay in touch with your customer, unlike traditional forms of advertising. If they follow you on Twitter you can stay in touch with your customers well after they have left your establishment.

Social media marketing harnesses the power of peer recommendation

The majority of people trust recommendations by others. Social media marketing is the only media that can harness the most powerful form of advertising, word of mouth, by making it possible for consumers to communicate with each other and vote for products or services by pressing the 'like' or 'follow' button.

Helps builds your brand

Never has there been so much opportunity to build your brand. Your brand is simply the most valuable asset of your business. Your brand is what differentiates you from other businesses, it is the image people have of your business and it establishes loyalty. With social media you have the opportunity to engage with consumers and build positive brand associations in a way that no other media can. Consumers now have the choice and opportunity to follow your brand and if they do, this means they actually want to hear or see what you have to say.

Humanises your brand

Social media allows you to communicate with your audience in a totally unique way. Your brand is no longer a rigid logo but a personality, not only can you show your appreciation and the value you place on your audience but they can also grow to love your brand too. No other type of marketing allows this type of two way live communication.

Offers continual exposure to your product

Social media marketing allows you to be continually in contact with your followers. Once you built your audience they can hear from you and see your brand on a daily basis. Statistics prove that on average a person needs to see or connect with a brand seven times before purchasing. This is a difficult and costly goal to achieve with traditional forms of advertising but incredibly easy with social media marketing.

The consumer has a choice

Unlike other traditional methods of advertising the consumer has the opportunity to be exposed to your product by choice, they can opt in or out whenever they want.

Your audience is relaxed and receptive

The majority of people are accessing Twitter account and other social accounts to be social and in their own leisure time. Social media is all about connecting with friends and relatives, meeting new people and making new contacts. People are far more receptive to hearing from a brand in their own time when they are relaxed, as long as the brand is offering some kind of value is not continually pushing their product.

You can continually engage with your audience

Social media marketing allows businesses to have an ongoing dialogue with your audience like no other media. Fans or followers who have interacted with a business on social media are far more likely to visit their online store than those who did not.

It's viral

Once your followers choose to interact or share your content then this interaction is seen by their network of friends who are then also exposed to your brand. This is how viral growth happens which results in audience growth and brand awareness, more prospects, more customers and increased sales.

Social media is an asset to your business

Unlike other forms of advertising where you see your marketing investment disappear your Twitter profile page or any other social account becomes a valuable asset. If you are using your social media marketing correctly your network will grow, you will be building trust and your asset will increase in value. With traditional advertising once an advert is delivered the connection with the buyer is over and you see your investment literally disappear.

It is like having your own broadcasting channel

Once you have your campaign set up and your follower numbers are growing, you literally have your very own broadcasting channel which you own. You can communicate with your followers about anything 24/7. Nobody can take this away unless of course you are not running it correctly and you are losing followers. If you provide content that is so useful and interesting, your followers will keep coming back again and again to check if you have anything new to say. You then have a following of people who will associate your valuable content and their positive experience with your brand.

You can offer your customers proof of trading

Having a social media presence which is active and engaging helps to reassure customers that your business actually exists. They can easily check, by comments left by customers, whether your business is reputable and trustworthy and they are far more likely to buy from you once they see your active presence on social media.

Improve your search engine ranking

Google counts social sharing when ranking your website or blog. If people are finding your content valuable then the search engines will register this and rank your site accordingly. Social media sites are highly ranked in the search engines and having a well optimiszd profile is yet another way of being found on the internet.

Opens up a worldwide playing field

It used to be only the large companies who could afford to build their brand and have the opportunity to access thousands of potential customers. Now everybody with a business has the opportunity to reach thousands of people both nationally and globally, grow their business and benefit from one of the most powerful forms of marketing. Having a business no longer needs be a lonely island, you literally have the opportunity to get your message heard by thousands of people through social networking.

Provides advantages for the consumer

With just a few clicks of the mouse or the tap of a smart phone, consumers can be in contact with any business very quickly. For the first time they have a voice and a very powerful one, their opinions are taken seriously, they are and valued whether they are in contact through customer service or just following a brand because they are interested. People are wanting to remain close to the brands they are interested in and this is shown by the continual rise in the number of people following brands.

You can listen to your customers

You can now hear what your customers are saying about your product or service and you can use this information to improve or develop your products and improve your customer service. This help your business to become more transparent and shows your customers that you care and value their opinion which ultimately leads to more trust for your brand.

You can become a thought leader

By producing valuable and rich content for your audience you can become a thought leader. Not only will this help if you are a personal brand but will also helps to build trust and reputation for any business or brand.

You can make a difference

With social media you can actually make a positive difference to people's lives. Once you know your audience you can provide content which is of value to them and which is actually going to help them in some way. Helping your audience like this goes a long way in helping them to remember your business when they are ready to make that purchasing decision.

Endless opportunities
Never has there been so much opportunity to have direct access to so many people and neither has there been so much opportunity for any business of any size to have ongoing contact with so many of their potential customers. This is a marketeer or business owner's dream.

IS SOCIAL MEDIA ACTUALLY WORKING FOR BUSINESS?

It is evident that the majority of major brands are running successful social media marketing campaigns. These brands are investing huge amounts of money, time and resources into this type of marketing, however you don't have to go too far to see whether social media marketing is actually working for business, simply ask yourself these questions:

- Would you prefer to buy a product if you knew that a friend or somebody you know of had tried it?
- Would you prefer to buy a product from a business or person that you do know rather than a business or person that you don't know?
- If you were thinking of buying a product from a business you had no history with, would you go and look to see if they had a social media site and see what other people were saying about their product?

If you answered yes to these questions then you can be pretty sure that social media marketing does actually work for businesses. It has to work doesn't it?

WHY SO MANY BUSINESSES ARE GETTING IT WRONG

Even though most business owners have heard how powerful social media marketing can be, the majority are still unsure as to how to use it to benefit their business. So many Twitter profiles have been created with enthusiasm only to be abandoned a couple of months, even weeks, down the line. Others are painstakingly posting consistently every day but posting the wrong type of content without a clue how to get their fans to buy their products. Many businesses are just paying lip service and seem to think that displaying a few social media icons on their site is enough to miraculously increase their revenue, and some are not even connected to any networks at all. Although on the face of it social media marketing seems free, it actually takes a sizeable investment of man hours, and if you are getting it wrong, you may as well be throwing a great deal of money out of the window. Here are some common reasons why so many businesses are getting it wrong:

Not 100% committed and convinced

Many businesses are not convinced that it actually works at all and therefore are not prepared to put in the time it to learn how to plan and implement the effective strategies it takes to build a successful campaign. As a result, their campaign falls flat and they simply give up after a few months.

Little or no understanding about how social media marketing works

Many still think that setting up a profile and putting an icon on their website is what it's all about. They may even post a few status updates and some pictures of their product in the hope that their website is suddenly going to be inundated with new traffic and that these new visitors are miraculously going to convert into customers.

They don't understand the fact that fans and followers are

worthless unless they know what to do with them

Just because a business has maybe 1000 or 30,000 fans or followers, it does not mean this will automatically transfer to their balance sheet. Fans are just fans, and as long a business doesn't know what do with those fans, they will stay as fans and not customers.

Not understanding the psychology behind buying decisions

They have absolutely no idea about the psychology behind how and why people make buying decisions and, therefore, do not know how to use this knowledge to their advantage in their campaign.

Lack of clear goals

Aimlessly sharing content on their network without setting specific and measurable goals is just a waste of time and resources.

Not having a system to capture and convert leads

Building a following is almost useless if those followers are not visiting the business' website or subscribing to the newsletter so that they can be converted into paying customers. Many businesses are still not making lead capture one of their main goals.

Unrealistic expectations

Social media is a long-term strategy. It needs to be an integral part of a business' marketing plan, and today, it's as important as any other daily task a business may undertake. It is not a one-size-fits-all solution nor a solution for overnight success. It takes careful planning and long-term commitment.

The wrong audience

It's no good having a huge number of fans if they are not interested in buying your product. There are even sites where you can buy fans, but if they are not the right audience, they are very unlikely to be interested in what that business has to offer.

Not enough followers

The majority of businesses are going to need a sizeable audience to make any impact at all. Although engagement is important, unless a business has a healthy number of followers, it's not going to be a great deal of benefit.

Not being proactive

Many businesses seem to assume that people are just going to press the 'like' or 'follow' button on their blog or website. Unfortunately it doesn't work like that and people generally need a good reason or incentive to follow a business, unless it's a very well-known brand.

Trying to push their products all the time

This is not what social media marketing is about. Businesses that continually push their products are just missing the whole point of how social media marketing works and will lose followers as a result.

Posting too little, posting too often, or posting the wrong content altogether

If you post too much, your posts will be considered spam. If you post too little, you will just be forgotten. If you post the wrong content, you will not attract the right audience which may harm your brand. The top three reasons for losing fans are:

i.) The company posts too frequently

ii.) The business pushes their products too much

iii.) The business posts offensive content

Chapter Two

How to Run a Successful Twitter Marketing Campaign, an Overview

ONCE YOU HAVE made the decision to be 100% committed to your campaign, you fully understand the theory behind it, and you plan and implement the strategies and tactics outlined in this book your business is going to reap the benefits and you will in time develop an extremely valuable asset. One thing is for certain: if you choose to ignore social media, you can be sure that your competition will not and you'll be allowing them to steal the advantage. Social media is a powerful way to increase your revenue by driving sales, increasing customer loyalty, and building your brand while at the same time pushing down your cost of sales, marketing, customer service, and much more. Now let's get started!

So how do you leverage the power of social media and put it to work to benefit your business and produce amazing results? This chapter is designed to give you a brief overview about what is required to build a successful campaign so that as you read each chapter it will make more sense. Every aspect of this overview and everything you need to do and implement will be mapped out in more detail in the subsequent chapters.

The opportunity to reach an unlimited number of new contacts and prospects is available to every business today. You can safely say that your prospects are out there and all you need to do is know where to find them, how to connect with them, and how to capture and convert them into your customers.

Successful businesses are using Twitter and the other social media platforms in a totally different way from traditional methods of marketing. With Twitter marketing there is no need to employ pushy sales techniques. Once you put the essential work, planning, and system in place, you will find your products are practically selling themselves and your prospects are buying your products and becoming your brand advocates as a natural progression from your initial contact with them. The whole process is straightforward and as long as you carry out the necessary background work, planning, and preparation, you can make it work for your business.

Know what you want

You need to have a very good idea where you want your business to be in the next one to three years. If you don't know what you want, then it is unlikely that your business will achieve anywhere near its potential. When you have a clear vision for your business, it helps you to focus and create the necessary goals you need to put into place to achieve that vision.

Define your business, brand, and target audience

Brands establish customer loyalty, and Twitter offers you a huge opportunity to build your brand. In order to communicate in the right way, you need to create and consistently deliver the right message and brand experience to your prospects and customers. To do this, you need to define your business and define and understand your target audience so you can create your brand.

Plan, plan, plan

Social media is not a quick fix. The majority of businesses start a campaign and then fall by the wayside. If you want to grow your business, then careful planning is required and it will involve creating your mission statement, setting clear and measurable goals and objectives, and planning your content strategy in line with who and what your target audience wants. Without a carefully crafted plan your campaign is extremely unlikely to reach its full potential.

Prepare your business

Before launching your campaign you need to prepare your whole business so your brand and your brand message are evident throughout. You will need to communicate your brand through everything your do or say, including all your marketing material, brochures, promotional material, your website, your blog, and your email.

Your website is one of the best sales people you can have. It works 24/7 and can help to make your business turn up in your customer's home at the click of a mouse. When your prospect arrives on your website it immediately needs to make them feel that they have arrived at the right place, that you understand their needs, and that you can either provide a solution or give them exactly what they want. If you already have a website, you need to check that it has all the necessary features it takes to grab your visitors' attention, deliver the right message, capture them, and convert them into customers. Statistics prove that unless a business has a clever method of capturing leads, the majority of visitors to a website will leave without buying anything or ever returning again. Therefore, before even starting your Twitter campaign, you will need to check or create your website so that it does the job it is supposed to, which is to capture leads for later sales conversion.

Set up your email campaign

Email is still one of the most effective methods of converting leads, and an up-to-date list of prospects who have given their permission for you to contact them on a regular basis has got to be one of your business' most valuable assets. Capturing email addresses on your website and through social media needs to be your most important marketing goal. Therefore, you will need to plan your opt-in campaign and set up an account with an email provider so you can continue to build a relationship with your prospects and sell your products.

Create your Twitter profile

Your Twitter profile will in many cases be the first impression your prospects have about your business and is as important as your website or blog. The aim of your profile is to capture your prospects so that you can continue to communicate and build a relationship with them through their timeline and through email. It is unlikely that the majority of your fans will return to your profile after their initial visit so you really need to grab their attention and make your prospects take action as soon as they arrive by following your business and perhaps joining your opt-in list.

Create your Twitter posting calendar

Social media is not like traditional forms of advertising, so frequently pushing your products, posting ads, and plugging your business is not going to work and is likely to lose you fans. One of the most important things you are going to have to do for a successful Twitter campaign is to regularly produce and post compelling content that your audience actually wants to engage with and share. Twitter marketing is all about selling without selling, and the aim of producing content is not to directly sell your products but to do the following:

- Boost traffic to your blog or website, generate, capture, and nurture leads
- Create brand awareness
- Constantly remind your audience of your brand so when they are ready to buy, they buy from you
- Improve your ranking in the search engines
- Create engagement, build relationships, and encourage your audience to share your content with their friends
- Support others by 'liking', commenting on, and sharing their content
- Stand out as a thought leader and build your reputation as an expert in your industry
- Create such good content that your audience stays 'liking' your page and continuing to read your updates, which builds and encourages brand loyalty.

Your content is where you can connect with your audience through their interests and passions. Your quality of content needs to be outstanding and you need to delight your audience with the best possible fresh, new, and compelling material. Excellence is what you should be aiming for with every update you make. The biggest thing to remember is that you need to tailor all your content to your audience's desires and needs.

Once you are absolutely clear about who your target audience is, what makes them tick, and what their values and aspirations are, you can determine what subjects and topics they will be interested in. The majority of the content you post will need to be about their needs and not yours. There is nothing more off putting and likely to lose you followers than continually posting about your business and shouting about your products or services. Of course you can do this occasionally if you have a new product or a special offer, but you need to be selective. Otherwise, your posts just become bad noise. Remember your followers are mostly on social media to be social. If your posts ruin their social experience, they will associate your brand with a bad experience and it won't be long before you start losing your fans and potential customers.

When you have decided on the subjects and topics you are going to create content about, you will need to create a Twitter posting calendar which will help you to consistently deliver this high-quality content. You will need to incorporate everything in this calendar, including any events you are planning, any special industry events, public holidays, blog posts, videos, and offers or contests you may be planning. You then need to map it all out so you know exactly how you are going to promote them on Twitter with the functionality you have available to do so.

Build a sizeable and highly targeted following

The main aim of building your audience is to grow a community of followers who are interested in your products, will engage with your content, and become advocates for your brand. In order to have any impact at all you are going to need a sizeable number of targeted fans on

Twitter. Building your audience will be an ongoing task, and it involves many different strategies which will be covered in this book. The size of audience and time it takes will depend on the time and resources you have available.

The essential day-to-day activity

To build a strong presence, trust, relationships, and reputation, you will need to be active and nurture your fans. Social media is not a one-way street. It's an ongoing two-way communication. It's about going out and showing that you are interested in what others have to say, and it's about building community and getting your brand out there in the most positive light possible. Here are some of the things you will need to do on a day-to-day basis:

> Consistently post high-quality content
> Follow your followers and fans
> Engage, comment, share, and reply
> Show your audience you value and respect them
> Follow influencers in your niche
> Deal with negative comments

Analyzing and measuring your campaign results

This book is all about how to make Twitter work for your business, and the only way you are going to find out if it is working or not is by constantly monitoring and analyzing your results. You will need to constantly check your results against the goals and objectives you have set. Once you know what is working and what is not then you can adjust and steer your campaign accordingly to achieve more positive results.

CHAPTER THREE

GETTING STARTED ON TWITTER

TWITTER WAS CREATED in 2006 as a social networking service and microblogging platform to enable users to create and send messages of up to140 characters known as 'Tweets'. The original founders came across the word Twitter and decided it was perfect. The definition, a short burst of inconsequential information or chirps from birds, but of course it has become a whole lot more!

The service gained popularity incredibly quickly and Twitter has grown into a powerful worldwide news service, it is one of the top ten most visited websites and is used by most journalists and the majority of major brands. Today there are around 215 million active monthly users and 100 million active daily users who are tweeting approximately 500 million Tweets per day and rising. When you consider that news often breaks faster on Twitter than through the media, Twitter becomes hard to ignore when looking to use it to promote any business.

According to a study the way in which people are using Twitter is changing and only half of its active users in the sample had posted a tweet in the last month. This suggests that the other half of its active users are simply using it as a resource for discovery. Twitter users are hungry for information and new ideas that are either going to make their business or life better. The great news for businesses is that the usage is becoming more commercial and there is a now a growing interaction with brands among the Twitter population. Statistics show that people are using Twitter to interact with brands, post positive comments about brands and also to ask friends for advice about products and services.

Smart businesses who have identified that their target audience are on Twitter are using its enormous power to find new customers, generate and convert leads, communicate with their existing customers and build their brand.

Twitter provides huge opportunities for any business to get their brand in front of people they would never have had the opportunity of getting in front of before. You can literally grow your followers from just a few to many valuable contacts, influencers and prospects in only a short space of time. However like any social media platform it has to be used correctly and launching in without a plan and information about your target audience is just going to be a waste of time and resources.

THE BENEFITS OF USING TWITTER FOR YOUR BUSINESS

At first it may seem hard to understand how a service that offers you only 140 characters to say something, could be such a powerful force for marketing. So that you can make the best use of Twitter and to help you identify ways that you can use it to benefit your business, you need to know exactly what its capabilities are. Here are some of the ways you can use Twitter:

- **Lead Generation** The main goal of any business is going to be to generate leads for conversion. On Twitter you have access to literally million of users and the opportunity to find new prospects is enormous. Twitter offers a very informal way of making contact with people and makes it very easy for you to gain attention by simply following users. As long as you have a lead generation and capture system in place your business can benefit hugely from Twitter.

- **To connect with customers** If your customers are on Twitter it is very likely that they will want to follow you, and Twitter offers you an excellent way to engage with your customers. By staying in contact with them you can continue to build loyalty, communicate new offers and when they start interacting with your brand their followers will hear about your brand too.

- **Branding** You no longer need to be a big name to build a brand on twitter. Twitter has evened out the playing field and has made everything possible for businesses both small and large and you can literally get your brand in front of thousands of people. Once you are connecting with customers, providing them with valuable information, answering their questions and taking notice of their comments and complaints you can start building relationships and brand loyalty.

- Drives Traffic to your website or blog By sharing and posting links to useful content videos, blog articles and other useful information you can drive traffic to your website or blog which can drive sales and generate leads.

- **Event promotion** Twitter is a great way to get the news out about your new event or Webinar. With Twitter's functionality you can connect attendees of your event which then helps to promote it to a wider audience.

- **Promotions, offers and contests** Promotions are a very effective way of building brand awareness and also building your opt-in list. Word can spread very quickly on Twitter so it's an obvious choice to use this platform to publicize your latest special offer.

- **Introductions to new contacts and networking** The potential for growing new contacts and connecting with thought leaders in your industry is huge. Twitter's search facility makes it incredibly easy to find people who may be interested in your product or service.

- **Helps to break down communication barriers** If you have found particular people hard to contact by traditional methods, then tweeting a message can work wonders and people are often far more likely to respond or reply to a tweet than a cold call.

- **Monitor real time conversations** With Twitter search and other online tools you can listen to what is being said about your business. Twitter is great for catching potential problems early and gives you the opportunity to fix them and turn them around to a positive result before they get out of hand. By listening into conversations on Twitter you can also discover what your customers like or dislike about your product or service.

- **Customer service** Twitter is a great way for your customers to stay in contact with you and because so many people have smart phones and can access the internet it is often so much more convenient to contact a business via social media. Whether you use Twitter for customer service or not will depend on whether you have the resources available to offer to respond to customers quickly. Many businesses use a separate Twitter handle for their customer service.

- **Boosts your visibility on Google** Twitter profiles are highly ranked on Google for both businesses and individuals, this is probably because the content is current and Google loves fresh content.

- **Publicize Testimonials** If anyone says anything good about your business or brand then retweeting this is great way of spreading the word about your positive testimonials and you can also save them as your favorites.

- **Post your press releases** You can use Twitter as another way of getting your press release in front of the right press contacts. There are very useful directories available where you can find journalists on Twitter who may be interested in your stories.

- **Helps you keep up to date with news and trends in your industry** Twitter is used massively by the media in all types of industries for finding and publishing breaking news, so it is the perfect place to find out about the latest news and trends in your industry.

- **Helps to drive traffic to your other social networks** Using Twitter to find new followers can be very effective way of driving traffic to your other social networks. You can use Twitter very effectively to grow your fans on Facebook.

- **Helps you find suppliers and vendors** Twitter is a great way to find new suppliers and find out about them through their interactions and current customer feedback.

- **Find out about your competition** What better way to spy on your competition! Following your competition is probably the fastest way to find out what is going on in your market and keeping up with trends in your industry.

•

Once you are aware of these benefits you need to think hard about what you want to achieve and what your main goals are for your Twitter campaign. This is incredibly important when it comes to setting up your profile and when you start posting content. This will be covered in more detail in the planning section.

SETTING UP YOUR TWITTER PROFILE FOR SUCCESS

Before launching into strategies and tactics and how to use Twitter it is a good idea to first set up your account and familiarise yourself with how Twitter works. This chapter is going to firstly take you through setting up your account and then give you a tour of the site and an explanation of all the common terms which are used on Twitter. So lets get started!

The great thing about Twitter is that it is incredibly easy to set up and simple to use. Once you have set up your profile you are literally ready to go. To join simply visit www.Twitter.com/signup and you will be asked to enter your full name, email address, password and username. When creating your password make sure you make it as secure as possible by making it at least 10 characters long and including both upper and lower case characters and numbers.

Choosing your username Marvellustweet

Your username or Twitter handle is incredibly important and is what makes up your twitter profile URL. You will use it to log into your account and to publicize your twitter presence on all your marketing material. Your username can contain up to 15 characters however it is sensible to keep it as short as possible. Not only is a shorter username easier to remember but it's also easier for other users when they are mentioning you in tweets and it will take up less space. Many brands use either their business name or a shorter version of that name, however, if you yourself are 'the brand' then using your own name is a much better option.

If you find your name has already been taken then you can add numbers or a popular keyword that is used in your niche. You can use capitals to separate words within your username which is great for making your username easier to read and stand out, it also helps to make it more memorable and therefore better for your brand. You can change your username as many times as you like so don't worry if you suddenly think of a better username after creating your profile. However once you have started tweeting and building up your following it's not good idea to change it.

Follow accounts
In the initial set up process you will be offered some accounts to follow simply pick 4 at this stage and you can go back later and follow more.

Add connections
You will then be offered the opportunity to add and follow your current contacts by allowing twitter to search your contacts. It is best to skip this until your account is set up properly.

Add your profile image
Your profile image will display on the left of your profile on desktops and laptops and in the centre of your cover photo on the mobile app. Making the decision whether to go with your logo or a head shot of yourself can be a tough one as there are advantages to both. Studies have shown that using a personal photo is more effective as people tend to prefer to connecting with people rather than logos. If you are your own personal brand then it is a no brainer but if not then you will need to weigh up the pro and cons. Using a logo can bring professionalism,

brand loyalty and reputation whereas it is more difficult to build a more personal connection with your followers. Using a personal profile picture will offer a more personal connection but makes it less recognisable as a business account.

A good solution if you cannot make up your mind is to include your logo and a picture of yourself this is a great way of pushing your brand and keeping it personal at the same time. This can be done very effectively by laying your logo either under, over or beside your photo depending on where you are positioned in the photo. First impressions count so you need to upload a really high quality image and if it is a head shot make sure your picture is taken in a well lit area and you are smiling. So many profiles have bad quality photos and they are either blurry or dark and this really is a missed opportunity to create a good first impression. You can upload a JPG, GIF or PNG of either your logo or a headshot of yourself. The recommended image size for your profile picture on twitter is 400 X 400 pixels.

Your Bio

Your Bio is a 160 character description of yourself, it is probably the most important part of your profile and what you say will underpin your whole campaign.

The time when your Bio is most likely to be read is either when you follow another user, they see your profile in the list of another user's followers or if someone clicks on your username in an @mention. The first time they see your bio is probably going to be the one and only time that you are going to be able to grab their undivided attention. This is the time when they are going to make the decision whether or not to follow you and this is where you need to hook them with your concise and compelling description. Your main goal when thinking about creating your Bio is how you are going to get them to follow you and definitely NOT to try and sell to them at this point.

Creating a well constructed, concise and interesting bio is a craft in itself and writing a good one can be the difference between being followed and not being followed. Firstly you need to think about what your target audience are looking for, what motivates them and what are the problems they have and how you can help solve them. When creating your Bio you need to do the following, all in 160 characters:

- **Communicate exactly who you are and what you do** This is so important because this is your chance to pick the right audience. You need to communicate what you do in the most inspiring way and if this matches your prospective follower's main interests they will be more likely to follow you. Try and include keywords that will help you to get found for your subject. This may all seem obvious but you would be surprised how many people are not specific and you are left wondering why you would want to follow them.

- **Add something personal or amusing** This is not only a great ice breaker but also helps you to stay in the minds of your followers and adds a unique quality to your bio. This can sometimes be the difference between a follow or not.

- **Offer them value and benefits** You need to make it clear how your audience is going to benefit by following you.

- **Get them to take action** This is could be the only opportunity you have to get your followers to take any specific action before you have to compete with their busy stream of Tweets from other users. This is where you need to tempt them with something valuable and send them to a landing page where they can redeem your valuable insight or content and then capture their email. A good method of doing this is to get them to ask you a specific question and then send them to a page where they can retrieve the answer. For example, 'Ask me what my best tip for success is?' This is great because it gets your audience to start engaging with you and mentioning you. Simple but so effective.

You may be wondering how you can fit everything you want to say in the 160 given characters so it's a good thing to create short concise phrases or use the pipe | symbol to separate phrases and abbreviations. If you need inspiration then checking out other peoples bios can spark ideas. The best thing to do is write a couple and then ask yourself this question, 'Would I want to follow myself after reading my Bio?'

Website URL

Working out which URL you are going to send your followers to is crucial to the success of your campaign and will depend very much on your goals. Sending them to your homepage may lead to fewer conversions since the page will probably not be specific enough. Many businesses make the mistake of creating a great bio but then send users to a cold homepage with little information relating to their profile, suddenly the experience is over and neither you or your follower receives any benefit at all.

There are great opportunities to continue the your brand experience and communicate your message. Remember people are on twitter to communicate and engage and if they have clicked on that link they want to find out more. You need to ask yourself this, when a follower clicks on my landing page what are they feel and say to themselves when they arrive? Are they going to be disappointed or feel welcomed and valued. You may want to think about a few of the following ideas:

Your Email Opt-in landing page If your primary goal is to capture email addresses then you will need to tempt them with a compelling offer, a free ebook or report to capture their email address. Customizing your page so it is exclusively for your Twitter followers will help to continue the experience and make them feel welcomed and valued. Try and keep this page as uncluttered as possible as capturing the email is the main goal and make it as eye catching and interesting visually as possible.

A Specific Twitter landing page Sending your followers to a warm and inviting page with a welcome message about who you are and what you can do for your followers is a great starting point. Again you can customize it so it looks like it is exclusively for your Twitter followers. Here is a list of things you may like to include on that page:

- Welcome message
- Profile photo
- Invitation to join you on other social networks
- Email sign up
- Your latest tweets
- Call to action
-

Another Social network Using Twitter to increase your following on your other networks can be very effective. For example, if your main goal is to increase your followers on Facebook then you will need to send them to your page and give them a reason to click the like button. You can do this by building a custom landing page with a fan gate with an incentive to click the like button. This way you can continue your relationship on Facebook and by email. There are numerous third parties that create custom apps like www.heyo.com and www.woobox.com and you can also send a direct message to a new follower to help tempt them to your Facebook page.

A competition landing page Another good way to capture emails is to send them to a competition page. Twitter allows you to run contests without having to use a third party app. However you do need to adhere to the rules of your country or region with regard to running a contest. More on running Twitter contests later.

Twitter landing page templates There are numerous websites which create templates for landing pages which can be linked with your email service provider. Sites like http://unbounce.com/landing-page-templates/ www.leadpages.com or you simply type 'twitter landing page templates' into a search engine.

Your profile name

As well as your username you will also need to add a profile name. You profile name is what is going to be displayed on the following:

- The top left of your profile page
- The first name you will see in Twitter search results in bold
- In email notifications that other users receive when you follow them

You can use up to 20 characters in your name and you are allowed to add spaces and capitals so you can make this name make more sense to other users. You can either match it with your username or if you are using a business name for your username you can use your own name which will make it more personal.

Connecting to Facebook

Twitter gives you the opportunity to connect your Facebook account so that your tweets will automatically be posted to your Facebook page. You need to think carefully about whether you want to do this or not. Twitter has a much higher tolerance when it comes to frequent posting and you can get away with posting far more regularly on Twitter than you can on Facebook. If you are planning to be a power user then it's probably a good idea to keep them separate.

Your Twitter Header

Your twitter header image is a horizontal banner which sits on top of the view that displays your tweets and spans the entire width of your profile. The image size required is 1500 X 500 pixels but you need to take into account that approximately 100 Pixels of the height of your header is taken away by the menus at the top and the bottom of your header so you need to make sure that anything you want visible is kept within the central 400 pixels. You also need to take into consideration that the areas on the far right and left (250 pixels on each end) will not appear on mobile devices and also your profile image will sit in the centre of your header. Since you have so much space you can get really creative here by using an image which will communicate your brand and exactly what you do. However, make sure you keep it consistent with your branding on your other social sites so you are easily recognisable.

To upload an image to your twitter header simply click the gear icon on the top right and then click on **Settings** and then **Profile**.

Getting your account ready for your audience
Before you start actively promoting your page you will need to breathe some life into your profile by adding some interesting tweets.

THE BASICS

Once you have set up your profile it's a good idea to have a look around and find your way around Twitter and your account. If you are not familiar with Twitter then here is a brief run down of the features and functionality available on Twitter and definitions of Twitter terms.

The Twitter Menu

- **Home** Your homepage is where you will land when you login into your Twitter account. On the right you will find a stream of Tweets from the people that you follow. You will also see the number of your tweets, followers and number of people following you.
- **Notifications** The 'Notifications' tab is where you see your 'Interactions' and 'Mentions'. It's nearly impossible to keep on top of everything that is happening on Twitter all the time as the noise of twitter is constant however the Notifications tab lets you see at a glance who is interacting with you, who has retweeted and favorited any of your tweets and who has mentioned you, it also shows any new followers. This information helps you to keep on top by replying and thanking those people and makes interacting very much easier.
- **The #discover tab** The # discover tab is found at the top of your profile and is a really effective way of finding people and

new sources of information that are related to your interests. You will find, Tweets, Activity, Who to follow, Find friends and Popular Accounts. The information here is based on the people you follow and allows you to discover news and stories without having to follow additional accounts.

- **The Me tab** The Me tab is where you manage your profile and settings, view the tweets you have sent, view your 'Favorites' and your 'Lists' and 'follower'and 'following numbers.'

- **The Envelope icon** This is situated at the top right next to the gear icon and this is where you can send a 'Direct Message' and where you can view the messages you have either received or sent.

- **The Gear icon** The Gear icon is where you find you Settings, Keyboard Shortcuts, Help and where you sign in and out of your account. Your settings tab lets you manage your account, design, profile, privacy settings, email notifications, apps, widgets and lets you add your mobile phone to your account.

Twitter Lists

A twitter list is a list compiled by Twitter users to group certain users together. Twitter lists are an incredible time saver and let you cut out the noise from your main feed and view tweets from certain users who you are particularly interested in. You can create your own private or public lists and subscribe to other peoples lists.

- **To create a list** simply go to your **gear icon** and then select **Lists** from the drop down menu and then click **Create list.** You can then enter your list name which is up to 25 characters and choose whether you want it private or public and then click **Save.** To add users to your list or remove them simply click on the **gear icon** next to their name and then select the list you wish to add them or remove them from. You can create a maximum of 20 lists. You can share your list with anyone, https://twitter.com/username/lists/list_name

- **To subscribe to other peoples lists** simply go to their profile and click on **Lists** and then select the list you wish to view and then click **subscribe** if you want to follow that list.

- **To view tweets from a list** simply go your profile page and click on **Lists** tab and then select the list you wish to view.

- **To add users to a list** Simply visit their profile and click on the gear icon next to the 'Follow' button and then click on ' Add or remove from lists' and then tick the box next to the list you want to add them to. You can even add people that you d not follow, your competition!

Twitter Language

- **Tweet** A 140 character post or status update which can contain a url and an image. Twitter automatically shortens URL'S to 20 characters.

- **Follow** When you follow someone on Twitter you are subscribing to their tweets. To follow someone simply click on the icon 'Follow'.

- **Favorites** Favorites are represented by a small star icon next to a tweet. When you favorite a Tweet the original person who tweeted it will know that you liked it. Favorites are a very useful because they let you bookmark content on Twitter so you can go back later to tweets and take a proper look. You can also use favorites to draw attention to your profile and to highlight great things that other users have said about you in their tweets. Favorites are public so anyone can see what you have favorited. You can favorite anything on Twitter and you can view your favorites any time.

- **@Reply** An @reply is an update posted by clicking the reply button on a tweet.

- **@ Mention** The @ sign is used when you want to mention someone . To mention or refer to another user simply add the @ sign before the user name. Using the @ sign alerts the user to the mention. The @ mention is a very important part of communicating on Twitter and is used to publicly direct a message to a particular user onTwitter. @Mentions are used to start discussions and reply publicly to other peoples tweets. You can use the @mention to thank people for following, to draw attention to a particular user and they are also a great way for you to get noticed by others. NB If you use the @mention at the beginning of the tweet it limits who can see that Tweet. If you are followed by the user and you mention them at the beginning of the tweet the tweet will only be seen by them on their homepage. If you mention someone who does not follow you, it will show up on their mentions tab but not in their tweets timeline . If you put the @mention in the middle of the tweet everybody who is following that user will see that tweet and this is not generally a good idea.

- **Direct Message** A direct message or DM is a private message. You can only receive messages from the people you follow and you can only send messages to the people you follow.

- **# Hashtag** The # hashtag symbol is often used to draw attention to topics and keywords and phrases in tweet. By adding # before a keyword or phrase you have the opportunity to show up in Twitter search for that keyword. Also by clicking a word with the hashtag it will bring up all the tweets with that keyword. Some words marked with hashtags may become very popular and become trending topics.

- **#FF** #FF Stands for follow friday and is a great way to build your following. You will see hundreds and hundreds of people using this phrase on a friday on Twitter and is used as a way of recommending your followers on Twitter to other users.

- **Handle** A Twitter handle is the username url. http://twitter.com/username.

- **Retweet or RT** A retweet is a tweet that has been reposted again and is used to spread news and share other people tweets. You can retweet by simply clicking retweet below the tweet or the icon with the two arrows. However, adding your own comment and personalising the tweet is always a good idea, this way you can point out the how the tweet is relevant and of value to your followers. To add your own comment you need to copy and paste the tweet into your own tweet box, add 'RT' and then add the @ sign before the Twitter handle and click 'Tweet'. When someone retweets your content it's a great idea to thank them.

- **Trends** Trends are topics which are identified by Twitter as popular and are based on who you follow and where you are located. To find trends click on 'Discover' and trends will appear on the left in a list. When you click on a trend you will see all the tweets including that phrase, keyword or hashtag. You can use trending topics as a way to get found, but your tweet has to be relevant to the trending subject or the hashtag. You can change your trends so that they are not specifically tailored to you by clicking 'Change' next to the word 'Trends'. You can see what is trending all over the world and in specific locations by entering locations in the search box.

- **Handle** A Twitter handle is the username url. http://twitter.com/username.

- **Promoted Tweets** Promoted tweets are tweets that a business has chosen to advertise.

- **Timeline** A real time list of Tweets.

- **Unfollow** To stop following someone on Twitter.

- **Twitter Mobile App** Twitter's mobile website lets you connect wherever you are and extends the twitter experience to both mobiles and tablets. It's a great way of keeping up with your following and communicating on the go. You can navigate very much like you would do on your desktop or laptop. The app has the following menu items: **Home, Connect, Discover** and **Me** and you can do everything you would do on your desktop. It also lets you set up notifications if you want to be alerted to a particular user's account.

Chapter Four

How to Build your Audience on Twitter

TO RUN A successful campaign on Twitter you are going to need to build a sizeable following and this chapter is dedicated to the strategies and tactics you need to implement to do so. The opportunities on Twitter to build your audience are probably greater than on any other network. Because Twitter is an informal social network you can grow your audience very easily and when you follow someone on Twitter it is more than likely that they will to follow you back.

However because the audience on Twitter is so enormous it's even more important that you are very specific about defining who your audience are so you can build a highly targeted following. You need to be discerning and qualify users in some way before you start following them. When you know exactly who your target audience is, what they are looking for, and what motivates them, you will be more likely to find them on Twitter and create the right content for them.

Many businesses start by indiscriminately following as many people as possible in the hope that they are going to catch some potential customers but they end up running into a twitter follower limit with a following of people who are not in the slightest bit interested in what they have to say or sell. Twitter lets everyone follow up to 2000 people but after reaching that number the number of people you are allowed to follow is largely dependent on your follower / following ration. Another reason it is so important to follow the right audience is because if you decide to promote your account with Twitter, advertising suggestions are based on the types of account that you follow.

PROMOTING YOUR TWITTER PROFILE

- **Post your Twitter handle URL on all your sites** Make sure your Twitter handle link is on all your marketing material: your website, blog, Facebook and LinkedIn page. Twitter provides code for buttons at this URL https://twitter.com/about/resources/buttons. There are also third party developers that create plugins which can be integrated into your page, they also offer plugins for multiple social platforms.

- **Embed a timeline into your website** You can easily display your recent tweets with images on your website or blog by visiting this page https://twitter.com/settings/widgets . It's really tempting for your website visitors to press the follow button if they can see how interesting your tweets are. You can also embed public tweets from any user on twitter, favorites from any user, lists that you own or subscribe to and customized search results.

- **Add your Twitter handle to all your promotional information** Make sure you add your Twitter URL to any marketing literature, business cards, brochures, your transport, product packaging, storefront, receipts or anywhere you promote your business.

- **Invite your contacts** Send an email to your current contacts inviting them to join you on Twitter. This is a great way to engage with them and also increase your reach through their contacts. You can search contacts from the 'Discover' tab, simply click on 'Find Friends' and you can search your email address book and then follow them.

- **Invite your followers** Invite your fans and followers from other social networks like LinkedIn and Facebook by posting an image, invitation and link.

- **Add your Twitter link to your email signature** Adding a link to your Twitter page on your email signature is a really effective way of gaining followers, especially if you give your readers an incentive or reason to follow you by offering them something of value or inviting them to join for a competition or sweepstake.

- Add your profile to Twitter directories Directories like wefollow.com and Twellow.com allow you to add your profile so you can gain more followers. There are other directories too, simply type 'Twitter Directories' into a search engine.
- **Leave comments on blogs and articles** Leaving comments and a link to any of your related content and your twitter handle can be a good way of gaining followers who are interested in the same things as you.
- **Write articles for other blogs** Many bloggers are looking for other bloggers to write guest posts, this is a good way of getting in front of a new audiences who may have a similar interests.

FINDING AND FOLLOWING YOUR TARGET AUDIENCE

One of the most effective ways to build your audience on Twitter is to go out and actively find your target audience and then follow them. You not only draw attention to your profile when you follow a user but they are very likely to follow you back if they find your bio interesting. Once they follow you back you will be able to start building trust and building a relationship with your followers. When they start engaging with your content, retweeting, mentioning you and favoriting you, this will naturally increase your reach.

Finding users through Twitter advanced search.

Twitter has an advanced search facility that lets you search users by keyword, hashtag and location, you can find it at this URL https://twitter.com/search-advanced . It's a powerful way of finding users in your town or city and allows you to be very specific with the numerous ways in which you can refine your results. By adding :) or : (you can search positive or negative results. You can add more than one keyword by separating the words with OR and you can search for users within a specific distance of a particular location, for example,by typing in 'near: NYC within:15 mi.' you can find tweets created within 15 miles of New York City. You can even search for tweets which have links by adding the words 'filter:links'.

Twitter allows you to save up to 25 searches which is very handy if you want to follow a certain number of people in one day from that list and then continue again on another day.

Finding new information and followers with #discover

The #discover tab is found at the top of your profile and helps you to find people and new sources of information that have been customized to you, based on the people you follow. It allows you to discover news and stories without having to follow additional accounts.

- **Tweets** Tweets reveal headlines that are breaking on Twitter and those that are being talked about by people like you. It also shows how many times the stories have been retweeted or favorited by your followers or the followers of your followers so it's a great way to find other users with similar interests.
- **Activity** The activity guide shows you how the people who are following you are engaging on Twitter, and shows who they have favorited, retweeted and followed. This is a great way to shut out the noise, find out what's important to people and find new followers.
- **Who to Follow** Twitter suggests accounts that you may like to follow and they are based on your interests and the type of users who you already follow. You may find some real gems here so keep an eye out.
- **Find Friends** Twitter lets you search your email address book to find friends and this works with yahoo mail, gmail, hotmail and aol.

Your competition's followers

Following your competitor's followers is an obvious way to find your audience, however be careful as your competitors are not necessarily always targeting the right users.

NB Filtered Tweets

You can now choose which timeline to view when viewing other profiles: Tweets, Tweets with photos/video or Tweets and replies. This makes it so much easier for you to find what you are looking for and stops you getting lost in endless text.

USE # HASHTAGS TO FIND AND GET FOUND

The # hashtag symbol is often used to draw attention to topics and keywords and phrases in a tweet. By adding the # sign before a keyword or phrase you have the opportunity to show up in Twitter search for that keyword. By clicking a word with the hashtag symbol it will bring up all the tweets which contain that keyword. Some words marked with hashtags may become very popular and then become trending topics. Hashtags are often used for reporting especially during a disaster or crisis.

The probability of being retweeted and getting found is much higher if you use hashtags. By adding the # symbol to the name of a topic or subject you are more likely to get found by the right audience who are looking for that particular topic. When you have found the hashtag phrase you wish to use you can use this in your tweets and also use it to join in existing conversations on twitter. It's easier to join a hashtag campaign which is already running, but if you wish to create your own here are some tips:

- Find out if the hashtag already exists, the meaning it has (sometimes it can have more than one meaning) and the audience it is appealing to (sometimes it can appeal to a different audience to the one you wish to attract). www.hashtags.org is a site which will tells you if and when during the week a hashtag is popular and if the hashtag is reaching the right audience.
- Try and be as specific as possible so you do not get mixed up with too much other unrelated content.
- Use capitals to separate words as it makes it much easier to read. For example, hashtagsaregreat is much easier to read as

HashTagsAreGreat.

- Add your hashtag definition to www.hashtags.org
- Do not use more than 2 hashtags in a tweet.
- Set up an email alert so that you know when somebody uses your Hashtag. You can do this at www.twilert.com
- Write the comment before the hashtag to keep your audience interested.
- Do not over use hashtags as they can become very boring.
-

Hashtags to find like minded people

Hashtags are a great way to find active users who have similar interests so you can start following them, introduce your brand and start building a relationship with them.

Hashtags to chat

Hashtags are often used so people can get together and chat to people about a particular subject. Tweetchat.com is a great tool to use to chat on Twitter. Simply sign in with twitter and then search for your preferred hashtag and join in the conversation. Tweetchat automatically adds the hashtag to your tweet and you can view all the tweets relating to that hashtag in realtime.

MORE WAYS TO GET FOLLOWERS

Participate in Trending Topics

On the left hand side of 'Discover,' 'Notifications' and 'Search' you will see 'Trends'. Trends are topics that are popular at this moment in time. They are determined by an algorithm set by twitter that is based on who you follow and your location. When you click on a trend you will see all the tweets relating to that trend or hashtag.

You can change the location of your trends by changing your custom settings. Simply click on **Change** next to the word Trends and then click on the word **Change** you can select from any location, locally or worldwide.

Participating in trending topics can be a very effective way of gaining more followers who may be interested in your particular niche or industry . To do this you need to pick a trend that is relevant to your business in some way and then simply post your tweet and related content with the phrase or hashtag. It is against Twitter rules to use trends by posting unrelated content and they run quality checks so that any unrelated content will not appear in search.

Join #Follow Friday

Participating in #follow friday is a great way to increase your followers. You can recommend any of your followers. However do not spam your timeline by mentioning all your followers in a series of separate tweets. The best way to do this is to either Tweet about a single person or a small group to follow and give a reason, for example, #FF *#FollowFriday @Yourfollowersusername Tweets great info and a great guy too*. Another effective way to save mentioning too many people is create your own list called #Followfriday and suggest people to follow on that list.

Tweeting frequently and posting really good content

If you are tweeting frequently and posting really good content and people are retweeting, mentioning and favoriting you then this is going to increase your reach and will in turn increase the number of followers. This is a biggie and is covered in detail later.

RUNNING A TWITTER PROMOTION OR CONTEST

There are all sorts of benefits to running a contest on Twitter, including helping to build your audience, increasing your opt-in subscribers, building brand awareness and creating buzz. Before you decide on your contest you need to be clear about your goals, are you trying to increase number of followers, increase your opt-in list, drive engagement or promote a particular product or service.

Twitter does not give many restrictions with regard to running a contest but you will need to look into the Twitter rules and guidelines, the rules of your area or state concerning competitions and contests.

To run a contest you will need to think about the following;

The Prize

In order to attract the right audience your prize or prizes need to relate to your product, or service that you sell so you attract the right specific audience. If you offer something like an ipad then you may get a large number of followers but not necessarily the right ones who are going to add any value to your campaign.

The Type of competition or contest

There are a number of different types of competitions including sweepstakes which you can set up manually or by using and third party application like binkd.com . With these third party sites they will create a landing page for you with your company logo, information about the contest and prizes and they will also select a winner automatically after the competition has ended. Competitions on Twitter can include offering prizes for tweeting a particular update, for following a particular user or for posting updates with a specific hashtag. Other idea for contest include:

- **Follow to win contests** Follow to win contest are exactly what they say they are, participants are asked to follow or follow and retweet to enter. It's a good idea to use the hashtag #FollowToWin.

- **Photo Contests** With photo contests you can ask users to upload and vote on photos. Using a third party app like www.wishpond.com can help with the administration of these types of competition.

- **Creative answer contests and Q & A contests** These types of contests work well and are very straight forward however you should remember to ask participants to mention your username (by adding @ sign to your username)to collect entrants as hashtags are not guaranteed to show up all the results.

The duration of the competition or contest

You will need to decide on the duration of the competition. With photo and video competitions you will need to offer your participants longer to enter than if you were are running a more simple sweepstake.

Landing Page

For all competitions you should have a dedicated landing page which offers information on the prizes and rules. By using sites such as Binkd they will actually create your landing page and administer your contest.

Rules

You need to make sure you include the following:

- The number of times a participant is allowed to join or retweet
- The creation of multiple accounts that users may create to enter numerous times
- The amount of time the winner has to claim their prize
- The closing date
- Who is eligible
- How winners will be selected
- Include the term 'Void if prohibited' to ensure you are in compliance with any country or state regulations banning your promotion

Promoting your competition

To promote your contest you need to announce it on all your social networks, email your contacts and make sure it is publicized on your website and blog as well. Make sure you include the relevant hashtags #contest or #competition or #win or #PhotoContest or #FollowToWin.

Announce the winner

When you have a winner make sure you announce them via twitter, on your website or by email.

Measure your results

Like any campaign you will need to measure results against your original goals. You can use tools like Hootsuite to measure new followers or Google Analytics to measure traffic to your website.

How to Lose Followers on Twitter

You are always going to get a certain amount of fall out from your Twitter account, many will follow and then unfollow just to keep a healthy followers to following ratio. However there may be times that you notice that maybe more of your followers are leaving than you would have hoped. This could be due to any of the following reasons;

Tweeting too often Tweeting too often can be annoying especially if you are not adding any value at all. Tweeting 1 − 5 times a day is optimal but it if you really have great content you can afford to tweet more.

Pushing your product too often This is a certain way to lose followers. People just do not want to hear it.

Repetition Repeating the same content over and over again is just going to bore your followers.

Moaning and being negative This is an absolute no no and is certain to lose you followers.

Not communicating If you are not replying to messages or engaging on Twitter then you are not going to thrive.

Not following back This will certainly put many people off and they may quickly unfollow you.

Inactive If you are nor regularly logging on and posting then many will unfollow you especially with the availability of twitter tools which highlight inactive accounts.

Constantly retweeting If you are constantly retweeting others and do not have your own content then this will probably lose you followers. On the other hand if you never retweet anybody then this is not going to do you any favours either.

CHAPTER FIVE

GROW YOUR FOLLOWERS WITH TWITTER ADS

TWITTER HAS THREE choices for advertising, Promoted Accounts, Promoted Tweets and Promoted Trends. Promoted tweets and promoted accounts are self service advertising and advertising in both cases can be targeted by location and interests. Promoted Trends are reserved for brands with large advertising budgets and are managed by Twitter's advertising department. To access Twitter advertising simply go to the gear icon on the top right and click on **'Twitter Ads'.**

PROMOTED ACCOUNTS

Promoted accounts will expose your profile to a larger number of people and are a great way to increase your follower numbers. Once you have new followers you have the opportunity to generate leads, build trust, drive website traffic and increase brand awareness. Twitter determines who your profile is exposed to by selecting the type of accounts that would be interested, based on your current followers. You can also target your adverts by location, interest, usernames and gender.

Promoted accounts are displayed in the 'Who to follow' widget on the left hand side of your homepage and on 'Notifications' and on the 'Who to follow' page. They also appear on search pages and on profile pages as part of the 'similar to you' widget. As with most social media advertising you set your budget and you only pay for results so you only pay when targeted users actually follow you. Promoted accounts are a great way of standing out from the crowd and really do get your account noticed.

PROMOTED TWEETS

Another way to advertise on Twitter is by promoting your tweets. Promoted tweets are normal tweets that will be seen by a wider audience and are displayed at the top of relevant search results and will appear in a user's timeline just once. Twitter will only allow promoted tweets to appear in the users timeline if the Tweet is going to be of interest or relevance to the user.

To get the best out of promoted tweets you need to decide what your goal is and then drive results by including a call to action. You could use promoted tweets to do any of the following:

- Drive traffic to your website or blog with a link to your best content and you opt-in sign up form
- Offer coupons and deals
- Generate leads using lead generation cards
- Promote sales and special offers
- Promote a competition
- Promote your event or a new product
- Put yourself in front of key influencers

Creating your Promoted Tweet campaign

Creating your campaign is very straight forward. Simply name your campaign and then select how you want to target either by keyword, interest or specific accounts and by location.

You can either manually select the tweets you want to promote or Twitter will automatically select 5 of your most engaging tweets. You can customize where you want your tweet to be promoted, in user's timelines or in search results or both and you can select which devices to appear on and the audience gender you wish to target. You then need to set your total budget for your campaign and a daily budget and set the maximum amount you are willing to spend per engagement. You only pay for results including: if the user clicks on your tweet, follows you, favorites, retweets or replies to your tweet.

PROMOTED TRENDS

Promoted trends appear at the top of trending topics. When a user clicks on a promoted trend they will see all the tweets relating to that trending topic with the advertisers tweets at the top. Promoted trends offer massive exposure but are really only relevant to businesses with huge advertising budgets.

TWITTER LEAD GENERATION CARDS

Twitter lead generation cards are now available to all businesses. They help you to get more from your promoted tweets by helping you to capture leads with a form which is situated within a user's timeline. They are like an embedded landing page within Twitter. When the user expands the tweet they will see a description of the offer and a call to action, their username and email will already be pre-filled on the cards. The great thing about cards is users can do all this without having to leave twitter and they can securely leave their email address. Some businesses have found them very effective at capturing email addresses of contest entrants.

Before you get started make sure you are clear about your goals and why you want to collect the leads. You may want to generate new leads for an ebook, or more subscribers for your opt-in, or you may wish to collect entries for a contest, or promote a special offer.

Set up is very straight forward. Simply click on the 'Creatives' tab and then click on 'Cards' and then 'Create Lead Generation Card'. Here you can add a compelling image (150 X 600 px), a short description, a call to action and a URL and your privacy policy URL. You need to make it very clear in your description how users will benefit and your image should demonstrate the value you are offering. Once you have saved your card and started your campaign your leads will be collected within your

Twitter ads account. You can download your leads at any time. If you have a CRM system (customer relationship management system) or an email service provider like www.mailchimp.com you will need to integrate and sync with them. To sync properly you will need to make sure your custom fields names match. Once set up, your leads will be uploaded directly to your database. Once you have the user's email you can follow up with them by email about the products they are interested in, or add them to your opt-in list.

Twitter provides you with useful card analytics such as a cost per lead card which can help you optimize your card designs.

CHAPTER SIX

CONTENT IS KING ON TWITTER

IN ORDER TO build a thriving community of brand advocates and customers who want to share your content, sign up to your newsletter and buy your products you are going to need to build trust, loyalty and likeability. The only way to do this is by communicating with them on a regular basis in the right way and by consistently delivering the highest possible quality content which will grab their attention, appeal to their interests and add real value to their lives. Once your followers start engaging with your content, you will start building trust and start converting them into customers.

Content really is king on Twitter and in order to create the right content you are going to need to have a real understanding of your target audience and deep insight into what interests and motivates them. Once you have this information and put this together with the strategies in this book and there is no reason why you cannot build a thriving community of advocates for your brand on Twitter. In this chapter you are going to learn about the different types of content, the different types of media you can use and tips on how to create the best experience for the followers so you can receive the highest engagement.

29 IDEAS FOR CREATING CONTENT ON TWITTER

You may be wondering how you are going to consistently produce and deliver compelling content to your audience on a regular basis for the foreseeable future. However, once you have picked your topic of interest, you will surprised how one idea lead will lead to another and you will be able to find numerous pieces of content to create and post. Here are some ideas for content that can be adapted to any type of business or topic:

1. Relatable content

Relatable content is one of the best types of content and one of the most shared types of content. Relatable content is anything that your target audience can relate to and identify with, it's when your audience sees a piece of content and immediately thinks, "Yes, I know exactly what they mean by that and that is exactly how I feel when that happens." It's incredibly powerful because this content is immediately communicating to your audience that you understand them and you feel their pain or joy and you can empathise with them. With relatable content you are communicating with them on quite a deep level which all helps to build relationships and trust. This is why Someecards is so successful, most of their content is relatable.

2. Emotive content

Evoking an emotional response is an essential ingredient to successful viral content marketing. If you create content that evokes a strong positive emotional response it will help your audience associate that emotion with your brand. Content like this is very memorable and if you can make people feel something by posting an image, text or a video this can really help in building your brand and creating powerful associations. Evoking any of the primary emotions be it surprise, joy, fear, sadness, anger or disgust is a certain way to get people sharing your content.

3. Educational content

Posting informative content about your subject is invaluable, this will help you to stand out as a thought leader and expert in your field. If your content is valuable and useful then your followers are likely to keep coming back for more and are likely to share your content too. Remember your audience are looking to find and share valuable content with their friends and customers too and will want to be associated with any compelling content you create.

2. Informative

This could be about letting your followers know about something that is happening like a Webinar, a trade show or n event in the area, or a special offer, or any information that will be of use or value to them.

3. Entertaining/amusing content

Social media is all about being social and having fun, people love sharing funny stuff. Even if you did not create it yourself but you think it is going to appeal to your target audience then share it. The aim here is to amuse and entertain your audience, humor is a winner all round and not only does humor break down barriers it is also more likely to be liked and shared.

4. Seasonal Content

Posting content relating to important holidays and annual celebrations is a really good way to stay connected with your audience. If you have an international audience then being aware of their holidays and religious celebrations will go a long way in building relationships.

5. Inspiring and motivational content

The truth is everyone has a bad day sometimes and needs a little bit of motivation or cheering up. A motivational quote will help to lift your audience and can really help to connect with them. If you know what your audience wants, what they aspire to and what their frustrations are then it is likely that you will be able to motivate them by posting content which inspires them. These types of post are also very shareable especially if put together with a colorful and inspiring image like a cartoon or photo.

6. Employee and behind the scenes content

If you have news about your employees and the great things they are doing then post it. Maybe they have been involved in a fundraiser or they have won an employee of the month award. Giving your audience a behind the scenes view of your business helps to keep your business and brand looking real and authentic and it adds human interest.

7. Customer Content

Having a follower of the month or including news or content about a customer's business is a great way to spark interest in your posts. Sharing a customer's content not only shows you value your audience but can also encourage them to do the same. You can also offer to mention your followers on #Follow Friday or add to a 'Follow Friday list'. This is a great way of offering them value, it also creates loyalty and keeps your Twitter account in their mind.

8. Shared Content

Whilst it's great to post your own content, don't be afraid to share other peoples content as long as it is relevant. The more valuable content you share the more valuable you will become to your audience and the more likely they will keep coming back for more. Sharing content is also incredibly important in building relationships with your followers, they are going to be far more open to your brand if you are supporting theirs. As long as you are giving your audience good content then it does not matter where it is coming from. You do not necessarily need to retweet all the time either, you can add your own comment and post a link to any piece of content you want.

9. Statistics

People love statistics which relate to their niche. If your business is B2B then posting statistics can gain a great deal of interest especially if they are displayed in a visually appealing way like with an infographic or graph. They are often shared if they are translated into a useful tip for your followers.

10. Questions

Asking questions about subjects that your audience may be interested in is a great way to encourage comments, interaction and community. People love to share their opinions and thoughts and love the opportunity to communicate, contribute and be heard. Even if you are posting an image or video it's a really good practice to ask a question.

11. Top Ten lists

People love lists about who or what is top or best. Lists spark interest and this is most probably because people like to compare their choices and judgement with others. Some may like to see that their opinions match others and feel they are right in that choice or others may feel comforted by the fact their choices are not the same and they are unique. You can create your own lists on list.ly and also get your users to join in by adding to the list which is a great way to increase engagement.

12. Controversial

Posting a controversial statement can spark great conversation and interaction, remember people love to voice their opinions, have an input and be heard. It may be a good idea to stay out of the discussion here as you do not want to lose followers and you need to be sensitive to your audience in order not to upset them so be careful with what topics you pick.

13. Special offers

Twitter is a great way to get the message out about the special offers you have running, but you will need to be careful not to post them too often or they just appear like advertising and bad noise in your audience's news feed. You need to make sure that what you are offering is of real value, that it is exclusive to your followers and you are offering them a deadline to redeem the offer.

14. Contests and sweepstakes

Contests and sweepstakes are always a great way to gain popularity, grow your audience, build your brand and build your opt-in email list. With contests your audience can have great fun with your brand and they can also create high levels of engagement. There are so many different types of contests: photo and video competitions, sweepstakes, comment to win, polls, caption this contest, photo contest and quizzes and the list goes on.

15. Voting polls & customer feedback

Creating a poll is a great way to encourage engagement on social media . Incorporating polls into your Twitter strategy can help to give you a deeper understanding of your audience and also offers you valuable feedback about products or services. There are apps you can use to help administer your poll like www.Polldaddy.com or www.polleverywhere.com .

16. Tips and tricks

Offering a weekly or daily 'Top Tip' can keep your audience hooked and returning again and again for the latest information and are a great way to increase loyalty and build relationships. Tips can be anything from instructions on how to do something, to information about a useful app.

17. News and current events

Offering information about the latest news in your area or industry is a certain way to keep people interested and sharing your content. Being current and up to date with local news is really useful to your audience and it keeps your business looking fresh and up to date. To keep up to date with news subscribe to news feeds and blogs that offer news on your industry or your local area.

18. Negative content

People always like to hear about what not to do, for example: 10 Things not to do on a first date or 10 things not to say in a job interview, the list of possibilities for this type of post are endless and can create a great deal of amusement and interest.

19. Music if you are a musician

If you are a band and want to promote your music then there is no better way to promote your material than by posting links to your music and videos on Twitter.

.

20. Q & A live session

Hosting a live question and answers session on Twitter is a really good way to create conversation and engagement. It also creates a professional, informative and caring image. You can do this by choosing a hashtag and then allotting and promoting a specific time hashtag for your followers to post their questions. When it is time to go, Tweet that you are ready to go and post an image, then do a search for your hashtag and check your tab and then start answering questions.

21. Broadcast live

By using an application called live stream you can broadcast any live event to almost any social destination. You can also watch, like and share any event that may be of interest to your audience.

22. Welcome Followers

Welcoming your followers in a Tweet is a great way of showing them they are valued. It exposes them to your followers which can help them to get followed and hopefully they will reciprocate and you in turn will be exposed to their followers.

23. Caption this

Posting a photo and then asking your followers to caption it is a really effective and light hearted way to drive engagement and you could also turn this into a contest. You can use images from stock photo sites or sites like Flickr creative commons, make sure to choose images that will provoke interest and are humorous or inspiring.

24. Case studies

Case studies are a really effective way to demonstrate how something works with real examples. You can use case studies to show how your customers have used your products or services to benefit them in some way. You can also use them to demonstrate a principle or method of doing something by using other businesses as examples.

25. Internet Memes

Meme comes from the greek word 'mimema' which means something imitated. An internet meme is a style, action or idea which spreads virally across the internet. They can take the form of images, videos or hashtags. There are plenty of tools and apps out there to help you create memes such as www.memegen.com and imgur.com which are popular ones.

26. Tweet a Pin

If you have a good pin or image on Instagram then tweet it.

27. Your blog

Creating regular blog posts is a very effective way of getting your followers onto your blog or website. Make sure you always include an image to provoke interest and asking a question can create intrigue and curiosity. Also pointing your users to other blogs is a great way of adding value and also building relationships with the blogger.

28. Greetings

Simply posting an attractive image or a wishing your followers good morning, good night or to enjoy their weekend will go a long way in breaking the ice and building relationships. These types of posts help to make positive associations with your brand.

29. Testimonials

You may have received a review on Google Places or Foursquare or simply a message from someone. Posting about good things that people write or say about you contributes to your social proof and builds trust. Remember people will believe more about what others say about your business than what you as the owner says about it.

THE DIFFERENT TYPES OF MEDIA

In order to create the best experience for you followers you are going to need to create a good balance of content using the different variety of posts available to you. Twitter offers you the opportunity to post text and images, and you can also post links to videos, podcasts, websites, blogs and videos.

Images

'A picture paints a thousand words'

If you are already a Twitter user then you probably know that an image grabs your attention more than any other post on your timeline. This is because most of us are visually wired and most of us can identify with an image much more quickly than text. According to statistics Tweets with photos receive 35% more engagement than Tweets without. Followers are far more likely to click on a link to a website or blog or watch a video if your post contains a picture. If you are posting a link to your blog or an article on your website then make sure you include a compelling image, you are far more likely to gain interest this way. Images not only get shared more, they also have huge viral potential, get remembered and also create an emotional connection with your audience.

With Twitter you can now really show off your brand visually and you can now include up to four photos in one Tweet which will be displayed in a collage in your followers' timeline. If they want to take a closer look they can click on each image to expand and images are even included if you get retweeted. You can tag up to 10 people in one image and names will be displayed alongside the photo.

You don't have to be an expert photographer you can find images from stock photos and also free sites like flickr (be careful to check the licence and what you are allowed to do with the images in terms of changing or adding text, etc.) Adding text can be achieved by using photoshop or other online graphic design apps which are available online and which are easy to use like www.picmonkey.com . Some stock photo sites also offer you the functionality to add effects and text to your images.

Your image file size can be up to 3MB and Twitter accept GIF, JPEG and PNG files.

Text

To ensure that whatever you are posting on Twitter is effective, then you will need to add an introduction or text of some sort. Posting a question can be a really good way of driving engagement. There are lots of tips in the next section about how to create effective tweets.

Videos

As with images video is highly shareable, has huge viral potential and increases engagement. People love videos and a good video can offer a huge amount of entertainment, make learning more interesting, more fun and easier to understand. Videos are also great at helping to build relationships, trust and rapport with your audience and there really is no better way of introducing yourself and building a personal connection with your audience than with video.

The type of videos you should be posting on Twitter are educational, informative and entertaining and while there is room for the occasional product video these really belong on your website and/or blog.

Blog posts

According to research 70% of consumers click through to a website from a retail blog. Blogs are nearly essential now for any business who wants to get found on the internet and social media is another very effective tool to drive traffic to your blog. If you do not have a blog then you need to seriously consider creating one. There are numerous free and paid blogging platforms available and there is a whole chapter covering this very subject later on in this book.

Infographics and diagrams

Infographics provide a fascinating way to present statistical information. They are engaging, very shareable, have huge viral potential and make figures look far more interesting and easier to understand than a list of numbers. People love statistical information relating to their interest because it helps to confirm or affirm what they already may believe and helps to give them more confidence in what they are doing or selling. You do not have to be an expert graphic designer to create infographics, there are numerous applications available on the web which can help you create infographics.

Podcasts

Podcasting is a type of digital media usually comprising a series of audio, radio or video files. You can subscribe to podcasts as you can to blogs and newsletters. For example if you download a podcast on itunes every time the author produces a new one, itunes will automatically download it. As with video they are effective at helping to build trust with the listener and can also help to make you stand out as an authority or influencer in your niche. They also encourage customer loyalty if they are produced on a weekly or very regular basis and are incredibly handy for people who are on the go and want to listen while travelling to work or on the way to a meeting. Twitter is to the ideal place to promote your podcast.

Cartoons

Cartoons work very well with humor and relatable content. Posting cartoons that your audience can relate to, can help demonstrate that you understand and identify with them. Cartoons are a great ice breaker and highly shareable as well. Once shared they are very likely to appeal to more of your target audience and are a great way to widen your reach. If you have an idea for a cartoon and you are not an artist them there are sites like Fiverr.com that offer creative services at very reasonable prices.

SlideShare

SlideShare is primarily a slide sharing site but you can upload powerpoint, keynote, pdf and open office presentations. SlideShare is a great way to communicate your message and very straight forward and easy to use. It is also another way to get your content rated, commented on and shared and your presentations can be shared on Twitter and embedded on your website or blog.

Ebooks & PDF Documents

Turning your content into an ebook is a great way to present your content and offering a free ebook is a really good way to build your opt-in lists and giving your reader something of great value.

Webinars

A webinar is like an interactive online conference or workshop. Webinars are a great way of interacting with your audience and building relationships as they let you connect personally with your audience. They can be used for presenting and training, selling a programmer or course or answering questions from your audience. They can be saved and listened to at a later date for anyone who could not make the date and time. Using Twitter to announce your Webinar is a very effective way to promote your online event and get people to sign up.

How to Create Effective Tweets

Getting your Tweet right is the key to maximising the full potential of twitter. When you are trying to direct people to a blog or article you need to make your tweet so compelling that they click on the link. Make your tweets unique, interesting and try and make them appeal emotionally to your audience. When creating your tweet you need to think 'excellence' and when you read your tweet back you need to ask yourself the following:

Is this going to grab my audiences attention?
Is it going to make my followers curious enough to click on the link?

Is it compelling enough to be retweeted?

Is it going to help me reach one of my goals?

To create tweets that really do work here are a few tips:

Use questions or interesting headlines to draw attention to your tweet Questions are a great way of gaining attention because it can make the user feel that you are addressing them directly. Here are some example questions:

> Need help with your .... ?
>
> Can't find that......?
>
> Want to find out more about.....?
>
> Wondering why your business is not ....?
>
> Are you tired of ..... not working ?

Write for your audience Write with your audience in mind by using words like 'you' and 'your'. When you do this it looks like you are directly addressing each follower.

Keep it short and sweet Shorter tweets are more likely to be read than lengthy ones. Research shows that tweets with less than 100 characters receive more engagement. The aim is not always to tell them everything in a tweet but to get them to click the link. If your goal is be retweeted then keeping your tweet less than 100 characters leaves space for them to add a username and a comment.

Be specific Be specific and keep to one subject, you have plenty more tweets to create.

Provide a link Try as often as possible to include a link to your valuable content.

Include a call to action Wherever possible include a call to action, for example, 'click this link' or 'share this,' 'Click here to download!' Asking your followers to retweet can generate up to four times more retweets but don't overuse it and when you do ask for retweets make sure it is for your most valuable content.

Use humor Humor is a great ice breaker and highly sharable. Twitter is definitely a place for humor and it is a fact that brands which use humor are followed more than those that do not.

Include an image where possible Simply click on the blue compose tweet button, tap on the camera icon and select your image.

Use hashtags Add one or two Hashtags relating to your subject and add them at the end of your tweet.

Use Lists and numbers Using lists and numbers can be a really effective way of adding interest to your tweets, for example, 10 effective ways to........ Or 5 reasons to .....

Include Keywords Try and include keywords in your tweets as often as possible so that when people are searching they will be more likely to find and follow you .

Is this relevant to my audience? Every time you post anything ask yourself this question and if the answer is no then don't post it.

Scheduling your Tweets If you are going to be a power user on Twitter and post regularly then scheduling your tweets may be a very good idea. Scheduling tweets is a great way to free you up especially if you are going away for a while or you simply want to stay on top of your tweeting. Scheduling allows you to be stay consistent and spread your tweets out evenly throughout the day and also free's you up to engage with other people.

Twitter has now introduced scheduled tweets exclusively for its Ad users, which allows users to schedule tweets for up to a year in advance. You can access this on the top left at the twitter ads icon and then click on the 'Creatives tab'. Here you can create a tweet and add an image, location or card and then you can either set as an organic tweet (without paying for promotion) or as a promoted tweet.

There are other online tools that can schedule your tweets Hootsuite, Tweetdec and Buffer, more about this later.

Chapter Seven

Communicating for Success on Twitter

CONTRARY TO POPULAR belief Twitter is not just a broadcasting channel but a social networking site. If you want to get broadcasted on Twitter then you need to get Social and interact too.

A great deal of this book has been dedicated to building your audience and creating high quality content. However in order to build a community of people who are potentially going to buy your products or start talking about you then you are going to need to get social, interact with your followers and nurture your following. When you are targeting the right audience you can be confident that all time you are spending interacting and communicating with them is going to create new customers and ambassadors of your brand.

To nurture your audience you need to value them by welcoming them, offering them amazing content, helping them by either offering them solutions or sharing their content. You can only do all this by communicating with them and this is where you can really stand out by building a real community with your followers. If you are really good to your followers then this will most definitely be reciprocated and as a result you will widen your reach even more.

The first thing you need to do is listen to your audience by reading tweets on your homepage and you can then start communicating with them. You can communicate with users and reply to their tweets by clicking on the reply icon and you can mention people by using @mention. You can send direct messages and also you can support your followers or any user by retweeting them or favoriting one of their tweets.

@Mention The @mention is a very important part of communicating on Twitter and is used to publicly direct a message to a particular user on Twitter. @Mentions are used to start discussions and reply publicly to other peoples tweets. You can use the @mention to thank people for following, or to draw attention to a particular user and they are also a great way of getting you noticed by others.

The Power of The Retweet

Retweeting is what has made Twitter into such a powerful social media platform. A retweet is when somebody shares your content or you share somebody else's content. Retweets look like any other tweet except that they have the retweet icon with the username next to it under the tweet.

One of your main aims on Twitter should be to get as many retweets as possible which will increase your reach . Creating valuable content and building good relationships with your followers by retweeting and engaging will help to get you retweeted.

When you retweet another user's content it's a great way to show support, get noticed and engage on twitter. It's very much like the share button on Facebook. People feel honoured when you retweet their content because it means their tweet has some value and their content will have more chance of being seen by others. If you want a particular follower to notice you then it's a good way to draw attention to yourself.

You can retweet anyone whether or not they follow you or you follow them. To retweet just click the 'retweet' button under the tweet. If you wish to add your own comment you simply click 'reply' and add the letters RT with the username and then copy and paste the tweet with your comment.

To see who has retweeted any of your tweets simply type

rt@yourtwitterhandle into the search box and you will see who has retweeted and then you can thank them. If you retweet anyone you follow you can see this in your profile timeline. If you retweet someone you do not follow this will show up on your profile and home timeline. You can remove a retweet that you have made by simply clicking on 'retweeted' below the tweet.

Use 'Favorites'.

When you favorite a tweet you are not only showing your support to a follower but you can also draw attention to the original person who posted the tweet. When a user favorites your tweet it you can see it in your 'Notifications' tab.

Sending Direct Messages

A Direct Message is a private message that you can send through Twitter. You can send a DM to anyone that follows you and you can receive DM's from people who you follow too. There are two schools of thought when it comes to sending direct messages to new followers. Some people find them invaluable for welcoming new followers and building relationships and others are totally against sending them at all. It is a fact that many direct messages are sent out full of self promotion and as a result many people avoid reading them. However, for the numbers that do, I am of the belief that it is definitely worth sending a direct message as long a you are genuinely trying to spark up a personal connection with new followers and offering something of genuine value. Direct messages can be a great first step to building your opt-in by sending them to a custom Twitter landing page, or another social media platform like Facebook and offering them an ebook or report. Whatever you do, do not try and sell to them at this stage.

Auto Direct Messages.

If you are looking to gain a high volume of followers and feel you do not have the time or resources to send a DM to all your new followers then using an automated service like www.socialoomph.com is definitely worthwhile.

Here are some tips for sending direct messages:

- **Make sure you are following them** If you send a DM to anyone make sure you are following them or they will be unable to send you a message back. Also it really looks impolite if you have sent them a message but have not even bothered to follow them, they will be quite likely to unfollow you immediately.
- **Be Personal** Wherever possible try and make your messages as personal as possible. You can do this by using their name or using the words 'you' or 'your', or asking them a question. You could also comment on something that you may have in common with them.
- **Be Original** Sending something a bit different from the norm is far more likely to get you noticed.
- **No Sales pitch** Do not push your products and services or they will be considered as spam and you are likely to lose your follower.
- **Provide value** If you do include a link then make sure it is worth their while and adds value.
- **Offer to connect on another network** You may find that you prefer one particular platform, for example. Facebook . Twitter can be a great way to find new Facebook fans especially if you have it set up a custom fan gate page and entice then to like your page with a view to capturing their email address.
- **Make it short and simple** Shorter messages work better and are more likely to be read.
- **Ask a question** This is a great way to start a conversation. Make sure you respond when they reply though. Encouraging interaction like this may lead to increased clicks to your website or blog.
- **Use a unique link** If you use a unique link you can track how many followers have followed that link and test how effective

your message is.

- **Monitor and change your message** The best way to work out whether sending Direct Messages is working is to continually monitor your results. If you do not thinking you are gaining then keep testing by changing the content of your message until you are achieving results you want.

- **Keep track of your unfollow rate** If you start to lose followers maybe you need to change the content of your DM.

- **Reply to direct messages** This really depends on how many you are getting but there could a great opportunity here to connect by replying to a user and thanking them for your message.

MORE TIPS ON GETTING THE MOST OUT OF TWITTER

Now you know how to create great tweets and you know how to communicate on Twitter there also are many other ways you can make your campaign successful on Twitter. To make the most effective use of your time the best thing to do is set aside a particular amount of time each day to interact and carry out certain tasks. Here are some tips on how to get the most out of Twitter:

Listen first before you tweet

It's common knowledge that effective sales people listen to their customers or prospects, they then try to understand their requirements or needs and then direct them towards a solution. This is the same for Twitter, you need to listen to what your target audience are saying which will help you to understand and communicate with them in the best possible way. When you start interacting with other people and their tweets you will find they will start listening to you. If you give, give, give on Twitter, you will really stand out from the crowd.

Acknowledge, communicate and join conversations

Make sure you build acknowledging others into your Twitter strategy. Make it a daily ritual to view your twitter stream and comment and interact with users. It's really easy to just add an @ to a username and acknowledge a user. Retweeting is a great way of recognising people and when you 'favorite' someone they get notified which is a great way of drawing attention to your profile.

Appoint and select your Tweeters carefully

Make sure that whoever you appoint to tweet, truly understands your business and your brand so they are able to communicate your brand's personality and voice correctly.

Tweet about your high quality content

If you are going to be successful on Twitter then you need to try and create as much of your own high quality content as possible. This could be anything related to your topic in the form of blog posts, videos, infographics, slides, podcasts, images or webinars.

Tweet quality and not quantity

The more you tweet with valuable information and content the better. How often you tweet will depend very much on the time and the resources you have to create valuable content but as a general rule between 1 – 5 times a day is deemed optimal. Certainly do not tweet for the sake of tweeting as this will not win you followers.

Use the Pinned Tweet feature

Once you start using Twitter you will realize how fast the feed can go and your best tweets can get lost. Twitter now lets you pin your most important tweet to the top of your feed so your new followers can see what you are about and you can display your most useful or informative tweet at the top of the feed. This is particularly good if you have found it difficult to communicate your message in the 160 characters provided in your bio as you can use the pinned tweet as an extension of your bio. The pinned Tweet also offers you the opportunity to highlight your most important offer.

Thank new followers

If you want to thank followers for following you then it is probably best to do this by direct message, this way you do not create unnecessary tweets and jam your feed with boring content. Many do use the @mention to do this but ask yourself this question, when reading somebodies else's Tweets when you are deciding whether or not to follow someone, do you really want to read a load of thank you messages.

Follow back

It's best practice and good etiquette to follow people back on Twitter. It makes for good relationships and promotes engagement. You can always unfollow at a later date if you feel you are not gaining any value.

Unfollow people who are not following you back

In order to help you keep a positive follower to following ratio you need to keep an eye on those who are not following you. Unless you are gaining any value then unfollow because they will see your tweets. You may also want to keep following a user if you really want to attract their attention and get them to follow you back and you can do this by retweeting them you mentioning them. However, do not overdo this as this will just be considered as annoying behaviour.

Participate in trending topics

Trending topics are highly visible to many people. If you participate with the right content then you are more likely to get found.

Be consistent

You cannot expect success on Twitter in a few weeks. You need to be in for the long haul, you need to be consistent and invest time. Many fall by the wayside but those who are consistent and continually monitor their results reap the benefits.

Be a resource for your niche

Provide as much useful information as possible so users keep coming back for more. This also helps to build your brand.

Help others
Helping others and offering solutions to their problems can go a long way to building relationships. You can find out by searching for your industry keywords and the word 'help'.

Reply to Direct Messages and mentions
Replying to direct messages and mentions is an essential if you want to engage, connect and start building relationships. It's worthwhile allocating a fixed time each day to do this. If you do not have the time to reply to direct messages then prioritise by replying to the most important ones, but replying is courteous and a great way to show your followers that you value them.

Follow influencers
If you follow the right people on Twitter you will attract the right people. Following influencers in your niche not only helps you to gain knowledge but also exposes you to their followers and more like minded people.

Constantly be on the look out
As you use Twitter you will notice who are the good tweeters and what type of tweet or information grabs your attention. Make sure you take a note of these really good tweets and attention grabbing headlines and see if you can incorporate them into your tweets.

Be positive all the time
Most people are not interested in negative information and moans and groans. It stands out like a sore thumb and is guaranteed to lose you followers.

Repost

Not everyone is going to see your posts all of the time. If you are crafting well written tweets and posting good content then you want to get as many people to see it as possible. You can change your tweet content to give it a fresh look or add a different image. Repeating your tweets at different times of the day is essential on Twitter and if you have an international audience repeating each post four times a day at regular intervals is a good idea. Some people may disagree but by doing this your posts are far more likely to be seen by more people.

Give referrals

The rule of reciprocation works here. Whatever you give you usually get back.

Use Twitter Lists

Lists help you to organize your Twitter stream. When you get more and more followers your stream can become very busy, Twitter lists allow you to keep on top of top tweets and content and filter out the noise. If your Twitter lists are organized properly you can really help to increase your exposure. If for instance you create a list of your industry influencers you may find that other people follow this list.

Make your last tweet really good

If you are do not have the time or resources to be very active on Twitter then make the last tweet that you post particularly good and make sure it has a link to a page which has both valuable content and a email capture form.

Schedule your posts

If you are planning to be a power user on Twitter then you will probably need to schedule your posts and there are many effective tools you can use to do this including: Tweetdec, Hootsuite and Buffer.

Automated blog posts

There are tools available which will automatically update your Twitter feed with your and other people's blog posts. www.twitterfeed.com is good for automated posts. With www.twitterfeed.com you can set up a free account and simply add the URL or the RSS feed URL of your favorite blogs. You can specify what you want to show in the tweet, how often it updates, whether you want to include the title description and whether you want to prefix or suffix the tweet with the username.

If you are choosing the right blogs that appeal to your niche then they are likely to appreciate the quality content. If you do not have the time to create blog posts on a regular basis but still want a regular presence on twitter then this is a great way to constantly feed your followers with quality content while keeping the feed active all the time. You need to be careful with this if you using this to post your own blog links as you may find that just after you post your's another post is submitted and your post is no longer at the top of your feed.

Don't feed Twitter to Facebook

Twitter has the capacity to tolerate more posts per day than Facebook. Feeding your twitter posts into Facebook will just upset your audience and is likely to lose you your fans.

Notifications

A great way of keeping up to date with the most important people or organizations you follow is to turn on notifications. Simply go to the users profile on your mobile and then click on the gear icon and turn on notifications.

CHAPTER EIGHT

DAY TO DAY ACTIVITY

THERE ARE CERTAIN things that you will need to do on a day to day basis to run your campaign on Twitter. It is a good idea to allot a specific amount of time and a particular time of the day to do this. Here are some of the things you will need to do:

Following your customer's Twitter

This is important if your customers are business owners themselves. Following your customers will go a long way in building relationships. By following you are showing them that you are interested in what they have to say and also helping them to achieve their goals by helping to build their audience. By setting up a special list for your customers you can easily check their tweets and support them by retweeting whenever you wish.

Showing your audience you value and respect them

If you value and respect your audience they will most probably love, respect and value your business. Be kind, generous, offer as much help and value as possible, reply to their comments and make it obvious that you value them and are listening to them. Don't be afraid to be yourself rather than a stiff brand with no personality.

Everyone is aiming for likes, shares and comments so if you are helping others out by commenting and liking their content it is going to draw attention to your brand and they are more likely to take interest in your content. This is one area where the reciprocation rule works very well on Twitter. Engaging with content will also draw attention to you and your brand and you will find that people will click on your username to find out who you are and are very likely to follow you. Be friendly to your audience, be chatty, authentic, genuine and embrace the conversation. All this will all go a long well in building a positive image for your brand and will set you apart from your others who are continually ambushing their audience with self promotion.

Following influencers in your niche

Building relationships with key influencers in your niche is invaluable. Not only can you learn from their content but also these people can have literally thousands of followers, imagine if they follow you back and then share your content!

Dealing with negative comments

Every business at some time will have to deal with negativity from followers. Hopefully if you have a good product then this is not going to happen too often. There are 'trolls' out there who have nothing better to do than post negative tweets, the best thing to do with them is just ignore them and block them.

However there will be real customers who have real concerns and complaints and may post negative tweets publicly, there may also be people who really want to lash out to gain your attention as quickly as possible and spread the news to their friends too!

You need to deal with complaints as quickly as possible and be as transparent and authentic as possible. The best thing to do is to apologise and say how sorry you are to hear of the inconvenience they have been caused and offer to continue the conversation and deal with their concern by either private message or telephone. You can then deal with this privately, give your customer the full attention they deserve and decide on your next course of action or compensation.

Check your lists

Make sure you remember to check your lists on a regular basis. This way to can keep on top of the conversation without having to read every tweet. You may not be following some of the people on your lists so this way you get to see what they are saying occasionally.

CHAPTER NINE

MEASURING AND MONITORING YOUR RESULTS ON TWITTER

MEASURING AND MONITORING your results and performance against your original goals and objectives on a continual basis is essential. This is where many businesses go wrong, they carry on aimlessly posting content without checking to see what is working and what is not. Then after 6 months or a year they wonder why their campaign is making no positive difference at all.

When you measure your results you will discover so much information about your campaign which will allow you to steer your campaign in the right direction to achieve those SMART goals and objectives and stop anything that is not working.

When you originally work out the strategies and tactics for your campaign you will be estimating what you need to do to achieve your goals and objectives. However as you campaign runs you will see exactly what you need to do to achieve what you originally set out to do. For example, you may need to increase the amount you spend on advertising to attract new followers or you may need to follow more people per day. You may very well need to change the types of Tweets to increase your number of retweets. Perhaps you need to increase the number of competitions you run to increase the number of opt-in subscribers. This is what it is all about, making your campaign work for you by constantly measuring your success against the goals set and then adjusting your strategies accordingly in order to achieve the results.

There are numerous tools you can use to measure your Social campaign including Twitter analytics, Google Analytics and other third party sites like Hootsuite and Buffer.

TWITTER ANALYTICS

To view Twitter analytics you will need to set up an advertising account. Once you are set up you can view the following:

Timeline activity dashboard. At a glance you can view your activity on Twitter, how many followers, mentions and unfollowers you have over time and also lets you view the number of interactions (Favorites, retweets, replies) you are getting for any tweet.

Followers. Followers shows you how your followers have grown or declined over the last four months and also offers you insights about their interests, location, gender and engagement.

Website. This allows you to embed code into your website so that you can view the traffic that Twitter sends to your website from your tweets.

GOOGLE ANALYTICS

It really is essential that you set up a Google Analytics account. With Google Analytics you will easily be able to track how your campaign is performing in comparison to your other social campaigns and Google Analytics will be able to give you detailed information about the impact Twitter is having on your business.

Google Analytics Social Reports

Google Analytics provides advanced reports that let you track the effectiveness of your campaign with the following social reports:

- **The Overview Report.** This report lets you see at a glance how much conversion value is generated from social channels. It compares all conversions with those resulting from social.

- **The Conversions Report** The Conversions Report helps you to quantify the value of social and shows conversion rates and the monetary value of conversions that occurred due to referrals from Twitter and any of the other social networks. Google Analytics can link visits from Twitter with the goals you have chosen and your E - commerce transactions. To do this you will need to configure your goals in Google Analytics which is found under **Admin** and then **Goals**. Goals in Google Analytics let you measure how often visitors take or complete a specific action and you can either create goals from the templates offered or create your own custom goals. The Conversions Report can be found in the Standard Reporting tab under Traffic Sources > Social > Conversions.

- **The Networks Referral Report** The Networks Referral report tells you how many visitors the social networks have referred to your website and shows you how many page views, visits, the duration of the visits and the average number of pages viewed per visit. From this information you can determine which network referred the highest quality of traffic.

- **Data Hub Activity** The Data Hub activity report shows how people are engaging with your site on the social networks . You can see the most recent URL's that were shared how they were shared and what was said.

- **Social Plug-in Report** The social plug-ins report will show you which articles are being shared and from which network. The Google '+1' button is automatically tracked but if you want to discover what is happening with Twitter sharing buttons on your site then you will need to ask a developer to set up your Analytics and add specific code to your site. Information on how to do this is available in the Google Developers site. With the Social Plug-in report you will be able to see which is the most popular content and then you can create more of this type of content. If you have added either the 'AddThis' or 'ShareThis' Plugins to your site they will also automatically report your on site activities as well.

- **The Social Visitors Flow Report** This displays the initial paths that your visitors took from social sites through your site and where they exited.

- **The Landing Pages Report** This report displays engagement metrics for each URL. These include page views, average visit duration and page views and pages viewed per visit.

- **The Trackbacks Report** The Trackback report shows you which sites are linking to your content and how many visits those sites are sending to you. This can help you to work out which sort of content is the most successful so you can create similar and also helps you to build relationships with those who are constantly linking to your content.

Tracking Custom Campaigns with Google Analytics

Google Analytics lets you create URL's for custom campaigns for website tracking. This helps you to identify which content is the most effective in driving visitors to your website and landing pages. For instance, you may want to see which particular posts on Twitter are sending you the most traffic or you may want to see which links in an email or particular banners on your website are sending you the most traffic. Custom Campaigns let you measure this and see what is and what is not, working by letting you add parameters to the end of your URL. You can either add you own or use the URL Builder.

To do this simply type 'URL builder' into Google and click on the first result. The 'URL builder' form will only appear if you are signed into Google. You then need to add the URL, that you want to track, to the form provided and then complete the fields and click 'Submit'. You will then need to shorten the URL with bit.ly or goo.gl/ . Once you have set these up you can track the results within Google Analytics.

OTHER THIRD PARTY APPS

There are many sites available to assist you with measuring and monitoring on Twitter like www.socialbro.com www.tweetreach.com and www.bufferapp.com www.twentyfeet.com .

Chapter Ten

Twitter Automation Tools

THERE ARE A wealth of extremely useful tools that can really help to put power behind your Twitter campaign. The amount of time you have available for twitter will depend on your budget and resources, but making use of some of the online tools available will not only save you time but also help you to find your target audience, keep on top of trends in your local area and also help you to maintain a healthy follow/follower ratio.

Tweetdec

Tweetdec is a social media dashboard for the management of Twitter accounts. It helps to show you at glance what is happening on your Twitter accounts by dividing information into easily viewable columns. You can create columns for mentions, direct messages, lists, trends and favorites plus you can follow and unfollow all from one place. To help keep organized you can schedule your tweets on tweetdec and it also supports URL shortening. With tweetdec you can even mute users to eliminate unwanted noise

Hootsuite

Hootsuite is a social media management dashboard that helps you to manage and measure multiple social networks. You can manage up to five social accounts with a free account. Hootsuite is designed so you can listen, engage, analyze and manage all from one place. Hootsuite is internet based so there is no need to download any software. Hootsuite allows you to schedule your tweets and bulk schedule with a csv file and it also has built in analytics so you can measure your progress.

Buffer

Buffer is a free online tool that lets you schedule your tweets and post to multiple accounts, Twitter, Facebook, LinkedIn, and Google+. Buffer offers automatic URL shortening and basic analytics. Upgrading allows you to add more accounts and schedule more tweets than the basic free account. If you are using Facebook as well, it is useful to know that you can also post to your personal profile as well as your business page.

Twitterfeed

With www.twitterfeed.com you can set up a free account and add RSS feeds and Twitterfeed will automatically update your timeline with yours and other people's blog posts. If you do not have the time to create blog posts on a regular basis but still want a regular presence on twitter then this is a great way to constantly feed your followers with quality content while keeping the feed active all the time. If you are choosing the right blogs that appeal to your niche then your followers are likely to appreciate the quality content.

To use simply add the URL or the RSS feed URL of your favorite blogs. It's a great way of offering your audience regular content as long as you are choosing quality blogs. You can specify what you want to show in the tweet, how often it updates, whether you want to include the title and description and whether you want to prefix or suffix the tweet with the username. You can also specify to display posts with certain keywords.

You need to be careful with this if you are posting your own blog links as you may find that just after you post yours another post is submitted and your post is no longer at the top of your feed. Make sure you only choose quality blogs and also that you do not choose blogs that post to often as this can be annoying for your followers.

Socialoomph

SocialOomph has many useful features you can utilize to offer a really good experience for your followers and effectively manage your campaign at the same time. It offers many features which can help you do the following:

- Schedule tweets
- Track and notify you about keywords
- Review and Follow back
- Automate Direct Messages
- Search with advanced search facilities

Tweetadder

To use Tweetadder.com you need to download, purchase and register your copy of Tweetadder, you then add your Twitter username and then authorise Tweetadder to use your account. Once set up you can use the following features:

- **Search** Tweetadder helps you to find and follow people who share your same interests. You can search by tweet or profile or location. You can search the followers of a user and you can also search Twitter lists.
- **List Cleaning** Tweetadder lets you see the users who are following you and then you can follow them back. The unfollow users section allows you to clean up your list by allowing you to search your list to see who is following you, who has stopped following you, who is inactive or over noisy. You can these choose to unfollow them if you wish.
- **Send out Tweets** Tweetadder has the ability to send out tweets from your account from a pre added list of tweets and can also automatically send out tweets from an RSS feed. You can also automatically retweet predetermined users.
- **Send out messages** Tweetadder can automatically send out thank you messages to new followers and send out direct messages.

Socialbro.com

Socialbro is a tool to manage and analyze your Twitter community in terms of where they are from, what they like, when they tweet and how influential they are. It helps you to find followers so you can target prospective customers and it also analyzes when your followers are online and when is the best time to tweet.

Manageflitter

Manageflitter helps you to work smarter and faster on Twitter by helping you find out who unfollowed you on twitter and finds accounts that are active and inactive plus it helps you to find new followers.

Friendorfollow.com

Friendorfollow.com is another site that lets you see at a glance who is not following you back with thumbnail pictures of users.

Tweetreach

Tweetreach shows you how far your tweets are reaching and provides an easy real time way of finding, analysing and reporting the reach and exposure of your campaign.

Twitter Directories

Twitter directories are a great way to find users and get found too. Twiends.com, twellow.com and wefollow.com are all directories where you can register your username and select the categories you wish to be found under.

Topsy.com

Topsy.com searches and analyzes any topic published on Twitter. It lets you pull data for any hashtag, term or username for you or your competition.

Twitaholic.com

Twitaholic.com shows you the top 1000 accounts on Twitter. You will find many celebrities and influencers in certain industries. It can be quite time consuming to use though as it does not give you any profile information so you need to look at each individual profile.

Whatthetrend.com
Whatthetrend.com tells you whats trending all over the world on Twitter.

Useqwitter.com
Useqwitter.com is a really great service that lets you keep on top of who is unfollowing you by sending you a notification email every week.

Trendsmap
Trendsmap.com is a great way to see what is trending in your area. Simply register and sign in with twitter, add your location and the trending topics for your area will show up on a map.

Followerwonk
Followerwonk.com helps you find new followers by keyword, location, URL and name. It also helps to analyze your account and give you more information about who your followers are, their location and when they tweet. It's really straightforward to use and you simply sign up with your twitter account.

Twitter Fan Wiki
Gives you a list of similar apps available to use with Twitter.

Unfollowers
Unfollowers is an extremely useful app that helps you to manage your Twitter followers. It helps you to distinguish those who have unfollowed you and then you can unfollow them if you like. It also allows you to follow large amounts of people very quickly and the 'Copy Followers/following' feature is very useful too. If you think that another Twitter account has a similar target audience to yours then you can follow their followers or the people following them with the Copy Followers feature. This app also allows you to quickly follow and unfollow people on Instagram.

CHAPTER ELEVEN

BUILDING YOUR BRAND WITH TWITTER

YOUR MAIN AIM through this whole process is going to be to connect, capture, and convert your prospects through your website or blog, Twitter, and through other social networks, and this involves the following:

- **Connect:** Your product needs to be the connection between your prospect and what they need so the first thing you need to do is connect those two things. In order to do this you need to identify who they are, find them out of all the millions of people on the Internet, and then connect with them by offering them something they want or need.
- **Capture:** Once you have found them you need to capture them on your website, blog, Twitter, or any other social media platforms. This is so you can continue your relationship with them either by email or through Twitter and communicate your brand message. To do this you need to offer them some sort of incentive so you can capture their name and email address.
- **Convert:** When you have captured your prospect you need to convert them into a paying customer by nurturing them and continuing to build a relationship by offering them the content they want through email and Twitter and then moving them toward signing up for a special or exclusive offer.

To achieve this successfully you are going to need to have a well-defined brand, and that brand needs to be communicated through everything you do or say through Twitter, your website, blog, and your email campaign.

Whether you are a one person small business, a large corporation, or an organization, your brand is one of the most important attributes of your business. Your brand is what you want your prospects and customers to respect, trust, and fall in love with so they will buy and continue to buy your products and services. Your brand is what is going to set you apart from any other business and what will give your business the competitive edge.

Never has there been a better time for your business to build your brand and communicate your brand message to your target audience than through Twitter. Your brand is the main ingredient for success, and Twitter is giving you the channel to communicate it. You can literally communicate with your audience every day. If you get it right and connect the right brand experience with the right target audience, you are onto an all-around winner.

It may be that you have a well-established brand already or maybe you have not created your brand yet or it just needs some tweaking or fine tuning. Maybe you are not exactly sure what your brand is, or you feel it needs a complete overhaul. Whatever your situation is, you need to know that your brand is going to underpin your whole Twitter campaign, and it needs to be strong, clear, well-defined, and consistent. Once defined, your business is going to create it, be it, communicate it, display it, picture it, speak it, promote it, and most of all, be true to it. This chapter is going to take you through everything you need know and do to define and create your brand so you can get into the hearts and minds of your target audience by communicating the right message and brand experience.

There are many definitions of the word brand but this is the one I like best because it incorporates pretty much all the necessary information you will need to help you to define your own brand.

Brand, the definition

Your brand is more than a name, symbol, or logo. It is your commitment and your promise to your customer. Your brand is the defined personality of either yourself as an individual brand or your product, service, company, or organization. It's what sets you apart and differentiates your business from your competition and any other business. Your brand is created and influenced by your vision and everything you stand for, including people, visuals, culture, style, perception, words, messages, PR, opinions, news media, and, especially, social media.

Why is your brand so important to your business?

Branding is important because it helps you and your business build and create powerful and lasting relationships by communicating everything you want to say about your product or service to your prospects and customers. A strong brand encourages loyalty and will ultimately create a strong customer base and increase your sales by doing the following:

> Demonstrating to your prospects and customers that you are professional and committed to offering them what you promise
> Making your business easily recognizable
> Creating a clear distinction from your competition
> Making your business memorable
> Creating an emotional attachment with your audience
> Helping to create trust
> Helping to build customer loyalty and repeat custom
> Creating a valuable asset which will be financially beneficial if you sell your business
> Creating a competitive advantage

To do all the above you are going to have to find a way to get into the hearts and minds of your customers so they will ultimately buy and continue to buy your products or services. Before launching your campaign and setting up profiles, posting content, and engaging, you will need to have a clear picture of exactly what your brand is or what you want your brand to be. You will need to define exactly how your brand is perceived now, how you want your brand to be perceived, where your business fits into the market, who your target audience is, and how you want your business to develop in the future.

To do this you need a deep understanding of your business and the people who are going to be most interested in your products and how you are going to serve them. When it comes to defining your ideal target audience, you need to work out which of your products are the most popular and the most profitable so you can focus your efforts in finding and connecting with the right audience and then creating the right brand experience for them.

YOUR VISION/YOUR STORY

If you want to create a strong brand, one of the first things you need to do is create a clear visual picture of how you see your business now and in the future. This is about daring to see what your business could be without constraints or limitations.

This exercise will not only help you work out what you want to achieve financially and creatively, but it also makes you focus on what really matters and will help you create your own unique voice and story. This is incredibly important when it comes to your branding as this is what is going to make your business stand out from others and give you that edge.

To do this, you need to get away from all distractions and think about how you would like to see your business grow and develop in the next three years. This is more than just putting a mission statement together. This is about your core business beliefs, why you are doing it, what you want your business to be, and how you want to be perceived in your market. To help you do this you will need to ask yourself the following questions and record your answers:

Why did you originally start your business or why are you starting a business?

How did your original business idea come about?

What changes are you looking to make in peoples' lives?

What are you hoping to achieve?

What aspects of your business are really important to you?

What are your hopes and dreams?

What is your definition of success?

What sort of turnover and income defines that success?

How many employees does your business have?

Why are you in business?

What are your core values in your business?

What impact do you want to have?

What influence do you want to have?

What sort of things do you want the media to be saying about you?

What do you want your customers to be saying about you?

How you want to be portrayed on social media?

How many Twitter followers do you want?

What markets are you in? Are you local, national, or international?

Once you have completed this exercise, you will have all the material you need so that you can create the unique experience required to make your business stand out from all the others in your niche. This is the first step toward creating a brand for your business. This is the beginning of your story.

DEFINING YOUR BRAND

Whether you are responsible for defining, creating, and developing your brand in-house or you are employing a local branding and marketing agency, you will need to carry out an analysis of your business to define your brand. Completing the following exercise will help you define and clarify your brand:

- A factual description of what your business is and the purpose of your business
- Describe your product or service in one sentence
- List all your products and/or services.
- What are the benefits and features of all of your products?
- Which are your most profitable products/services?
- Which are your most popular products/services?
- Who are your ideal customers for each of your products or services? (Consumer or business, age, gender, income, occupation, education, stage in family life cycle.)
- Out of these customers, which ones who are most likely to buy your most profitable products?
- Is the market and demand large enough to provide you with the number of customers you need to buy your most profitable products and achieve your financial goals?
- If your answer to the previous question is no then ask yourself the same question for each of your other products.
- Who are your three main competitors? (Have a look at their Twitter profile account.)
- What distinguishes your business from your competition? What special thing are you bringing to the market that is of real value? What is your unique selling point? What solutions are your products offering your customers that will meet their needs or solve their problems?
- If you are already in business, write down what your customers are already saying about your business. What do you think they would say about how your product or service makes them feel emotionally? (You may need to ask your customers if you do not already know.) What qualities and words would you use to describe the personality of your business as it is now? Here are some examples of words you may wish to use: high cost, low cost, high quality, value for money, expensive, cheap, excellent

customer service, friendly, professional, happy, serious, innovative, eccentric, quiet, loud, beautiful, relaxing, motivating, sincere, adventurous, amusing, charming, decisive, kind, imaginative, proactive, intuitive, loving, trustworthy, extrovert, vibrant, transparent, intelligent, creative, dynamic, resourceful.

- Now, whether you are already in business or starting out, write down all the words to describe how you want and need your brand to be perceived and what qualities you want to be associated with your brand in order to match the needs and expectations of your ideal customers. If you are already in business, hopefully this will be exactly the same as how you perceive you are at the current time.

- What is the evidence that backs up what you have said about your brand? This could be customer testimonials or any evidence about product or service quality.

- What is the biggest opportunity for your business right now?

- What products are you thinking of introducing in the near future?

HOW TO GET INTO THE HEARTS AND MINDS OF YOUR TARGET AUDIENCE

Your target audience is your most important commodity, as they are the future customers and ambassadors of your business. Every single one of them is valuable, and every single one of them can make a difference to your business. This can be because they are actually going to buy your products or simply spread the word by interacting with you on Twitter.

However, it's a big social world out there. The possibilities of finding new people are limitless, but targeting everyone is not the solution. The biggest mistake you can make is trying to reach everyone and then not appealing to anyone. Your first step is to identify exactly who the people are who are going to be interested in your products or services, and then you need to find out everything about them. You need to get inside their heads and work out what motivates these people, what their needs, hopes, aspirations, fears, and dreams are. Your product or service is the link between them and what they want. When you know this you can tailor every single message or piece of content toward them.

When you know exactly who your ideal customers are, Twitter offers you the opportunity to go find and reach them. It's then up to you to capture them so you can continue to communicate. When you know everything about your customers you are more likely to speak the right language to be able to communicate with them and build trust to the point where the next natural progression is for them to buy your product.

It's only when you truly understand your audience that you can start converting them into customers. Once you know you are targeting the right audience, you can confidently focus every ounce of your effort creating exactly the right content, nurturing them, engaging with them, and looking after them. It's only a matter of time before they will buy your product.

Creating your ideal customer persona or avatar

The following exercise is absolutely essential. Your answers to the questions will be the very information that is going to help you communicate with your customer in the right way, by providing them with the right content and the correct brand experience. Once you have done this exercise you are going to own some very powerful information. If you do not do this exercise it is very unlikely that you are going to be able to truly connect with your target audience in the way that is necessary to build trust so that you can ultimately convert them into your customers.

Your answers to the questions in the previous section will have given you a clear idea of which types of customers you need to target to give you the best chance of achieving your financial goals. You now need to find out everything about them so you can get your brand into their hearts and minds. The best way to do this is to create an imaginary persona or avatar of your ideal customer and you can build this picture by finding out the following:

Describe your ideal customer and include the following details: are they a consumer or in business, their age, gender, income, occupation, education, and stage in family life cycle.

Where do they live?

What do they want most of all?

What are their core values?

What is their preferred lifestyle?

What do they do on a day-to-day basis?

What are their hopes and aspirations?

What important truth matters to them?

What motivates and inspires them?

What sort of routines do they have?

What are their day-to-day priorities?

How do they have fun?

What do they do in their spare time?

What subjects are they interested in?

Which books do they read?

Which TV programs do they watch?

What magazines do they read?

Who do they follow on social media?

Who are their role models?

What really makes them tick?

What are their fears and frustrations?

What are their suspicions?

What are their insecurities?

What are their typical worries?

What is the perfect solution to their worries?

What are their dreams?

What do they need to make them feel happy and fulfilled?

Big Questions

To answer the following questions you will need to step inside your ideal customer's mind and imagine you are them.

- How do you feel when you find your product or service? What is your initial emotional reaction?
- What are the words that go through your head?
- How can I justify buying this product for myself?
- Are you ready to buy immediately?
- Do you have any suspicions that the product may not be what it says?
- What are those suspicions? Why do you have them?
- Do you need more convincing?
- What do you need to convince you that the product is right for you?
- What do you feel when you have the product in your hand?

The reason why these are such big questions is because your answers to them will establish whether or not you have correctly defined your ideal customer and whether you have really understood their needs, desires, and fears. If you are imagining yourself as your ideal customer and you are saying "woo-hoo", ecstatically jumping up and down with glee, immediately buying the product, or relieved that you have at long last found the solution to your problem, then you have created the right avatar. If not, then you need to think again.

It's only when you have imagined yourself in the hearts and minds of your target audience that you are going to be able to connect with them on any emotional level. With the information from the above exercise, you will have everything you need to produce exactly the right content to match the needs, desires, and expectations of your ideal customer so that you can create the right brand experience and sell your products. This information is like gold.

COMMUNICATING YOUR BRAND

Once you have gone through all the processes outlined in this chapter you will have a clear idea about what your brand is, what is stands for, and how you stand out from similar businesses. You now have to work out how to best communicate this to your ideal customer so that when they hear or see your brand name they immediately make that essential emotional connection. This is what is going to make them eventually love your brand above all others.

When you are clear about what your brand is, what it stands for, and how you are going to stand out from other similar businesses, you then need to work out how you can communicate this message in the best possible way. Your main aim here is to create an emotional connection with your target audience that is going to help them grow to love your brand, remember your brand, and remain loyal to it. To do this you need to communicate your brand story through every aspect of your business, including your social media campaign.

With the information you now have you are armed with everything you need to create a consistent brand. If you have not already done so, you can either hand all this information over to a marketing agency or use it yourself to create all the following:

- **Your logo:** Your logo will give a clear guideline for all your promotional material, including your website or blog, stationery, templates, or any marketing material that needs to be created for online or offline promotion.
- **Your brand message: This is** the main message you want to communicate about your brand.
- **Your tagline:** A short, memorable statement about your brand that captures the personality of your brand and communicates how you or your product will benefit your customer.
- **All your 'about' descriptions:** You can communicate your brand story through all your 'about' sections on all your social

media platforms you are using.

- **The content you create for your business:** Every piece of content you create for your business needs to be tailor-made for your target audience. You will need to pick who and what subjects or topics you want to be associated with your brand, as anything you pick to write about will be a representation of your brand.

- **Your website and/or blog:** The 'about' page of your website is probably the most visited page on any website and there is a reason for this. People want to find out about your business and what is different or special about it. This is a great place to introduce and expand on the story of your brand. This is where you can really go to town and communicate your beliefs and uniqueness.. Also, the visual style of your website or blog and your individual voice should be evident throughout your site and be consistent with your brand.

- **Video content:** Videos are an incredibly powerful way of creating a personal connection with your audience. Make sure that whatever video content you produce and whatever you say is always consistent with your brand.

CHAPTER TWELVE

THE ESSENTIAL TWITTER MARKETING PLAN

BEFORE LAUNCHING INTO your campaign you will need to know exactly what you want your business to achieve and what achieve and what you hope to gain through marketing on Twitter. Without the necessary planning and preparation, your campaign is very unlikely to succeed.

The next few chapters take you through everything you need to do to plan your campaign before actually posting content. In this chapter you will learn how to create your mission statement, set goals and objectives, and plan the strategies and tactics you need to implement to achieve those goals. In the following chapter you will learn exactly how to prepare your business, your website and blog, and your email campaign so you can capture and convert customers.

CREATING YOUR MISSION STATEMENT

Many campaigns fail at the first hurdle simply because they do not have a clear idea about why they are undertaking in a campaign or what they want to achieve. They set up a Twitter profile and have little or no idea why exactly they are doing it. "Everyone else is doing it ... we probably should too." Then they launch in without first articulating the purpose of their Twitter campaign and aimlessly start posting content. Before long, they realize that this is having no positive effect on their business, and they either give up or continue half-heartedly.

Once you have defined your brand and your target audience you will need to produce your mission statement for your social media campaign. Your mission statement is vital for your business as a whole and for your prospects and customers, and it should clearly state your commitment and promise to them as well as communicate your brand message. You will be able to include this in your Twitter bio and on your business page. To create your mission statement, simply follow these for four easy steps:

- **Describe what your business does:** Describe exactly what you do, what you offer, and the purpose of your business.
- **Describe the way you operate:** Include your core values, your level of customer service, and your commitment to your customers. You can include how your core values contribute to the quality of your product or service.
- **Who are you doing it for?:** Who are your customers? Business owners, entrepreneurs, working women, gardeners, shop owners, etc.
- **The value you are bringing:** What benefit are you offering your customers ? What value are you bringing them?

Once you have created your statement, everyone will know exactly what you are about. You will know what you need to deliver to your customers. Your employees will know what is expected of them. Your customers and prospects will know what your promise is and what they can expect when buying your products and services.

SETTING YOUR GOALS AND OBJECTIVES

Setting goals and objectives is the key to your success on Twitter. Once they are set, you will be ready to plan and create the strategies and tactics to achieve those goals and objectives. You will be able to review and measure the success of your campaign.

Definition of a goal

A goal is a statement rooted in your business's mission, and it will define what you want to accomplish and offer a broad direction for your business to follow. The three main goals of any business will ultimately be to increase sales, to reduce costs, and to improve customer service. Each goal will have a direct effect on the others. Here are some examples within those three main goals:

1. To increase revenue and generate sales

- To increase website traffic
- To increase brand awareness through Twitter
- To build a reputation as an expert within the industry
- To build a loyal and engaged community on Twitter
- To increase the number of customers from word-of-mouth and referrals
- To increase the number of sales
- To increase average spending per customer
- To increase the number of leads generated
- To introduce new products
- To increase online visibility
- To promote an event
- To build a highly targeted list of email subscribers
- To connect with new customers
- To build trust and build relationships with prospects and customers
- To put a content marketing strategy in place
- To increase business in 'X' country/state
- To become a thought leader in your industry
- To develop new markets by introducing product into 'X' country/state
- To decrease spending on traditional forms of advertising and invest 'X' amount on Twitter marketing
- To build relationships with key influencers on Twitter

2. To reduce Costs

- To decrease spending on traditional forms of advertising and invest in Twitter marketing

3. To deliver customer satisfaction and retain customers
- To answer customer questions promptly
- To respond to customer complaints promptly, politely, and helpfully
- To provide online help/technical support
- To respond to customer feedback
- To listen to your customers

Setting measurable objectives
Once you set your broader goals, you need to get more specific and create SMART objectives (specific, measurable, attainable, relevant, and timely). Here is an explanation of exactly what each of those terms means:

- **Specific:** You need to target particular areas for improvement.
- **Measurable:** Your progress needs to be quantifiable, and putting concrete figures on your goals is essential for success and is the only way to measure the effectiveness of your campaign.
- **Attainable/Realistic:** You need to be realistic with the resources you have available, and the results you are expecting need to be realistic.
- **Relevant:** Your goals need to be relevant to the business climate you are in.
- **Time Bound:** Make sure you set a realistic time period to achieve your goals. If a time is not set then things tend not to get done.

Here are some examples of the sort of SMART objectives you should be setting:
- Increase sales of product X by X%
- To build an audience of X number followers on Twitter. within one year
- To increase number of followers by X per week
- To increase website traffic from Twitter by X times

- To increase opt-in list subscribers by X per week
- Increase conversions from Twitter by X per week
- To increase the number of leads generated from Twitter by X per week
- To receive X lead generation cards per day/ week
- To increase the number of new customers by X per month
- To increase the average spend per customer by X
- Introduce X number of new products every 6 months
- To increase sales from X country/state by X%
- To decrease spend on traditional forms of advertising by X and invest X amount in Twitter marketing
- Utilize Twitter to increase attendants at X event by X people
- Utilize Twitter to increase YouTube views by X people per week
- To receive X number of Brand mentions per week/month

CHOOSING YOUR STRATEGIES AND TACTICS

Once you have set your quantifiable goals and objectives you are going to have to work out how you are going to accomplish them using Twitter. You will need to think about the strategies and tactics you are going to use and they need to be quantifiable as well. Here are some examples of the strategies you may want to implement:

- To Tweet on Twitter 'X' number of times per day
- To retweet 5 users per day
- To get retweeted 'X' times a day/week
- To make 'X' % of posts photo/posts
- To create 'X' number of blog posts per week/month and post them on Twitter with images
- To follow 'X' number of new accounts per week
- To send out direct messages to new followers
- To post 'X' offers per month/6 months on Twitter
- To run 'X' competitions/contests per year on Twitter
- To post 'X' number of YouTube videos per month
- To follow 'X' number of influencers on Twitter per week

- To create 'X' number of online events per year
-

Of course at the beginning you are going to need to make an educated guess at the number of times you are going to need to do one thing to achieve another. As your campaign runs you will need to adjust certain aspects to achieve what you set out to achieve. For example, you may need to follow more accounts to gain more followers or you may need to change the type of content you are posting to increase the amount of engagement.

The only way you can do this is by constantly monitoring and measuring your results against the original goals and objectives you set and adjusting your campaign accordingly.

CREATING YOUR TWITTER POSTING CALENDAR

Now that you have your strategies in place, you will have a good idea of the amount and type of content you need to post to achieve those objectives. One of the most challenging tasks of your Twitter campaign is going to be to consistently deliver a high standard of content to your fans on a daily basis. You are going to need to post between one to four times a day. This does not mean you need to create numerous blog articles each day, but you are going to need to communicate in some way and find unique ways for your audience to interact with your brand and offer some kind of value on a regular basis. This may seem daunting to begin with, but you will be surprised just how one idea leads to another.

To help you map out your content for the next six months or the year ahead, you need to create a Twitter posting calendar which is going to be your key to consistent posting. There are many online tools and apps that can help you with this. Google Calendar is a very good calendar to use, and it lets you color code the different types of posts. You can also use Hootsuite, the social media dashboard, to plot out your calendar or use a spreadsheet in Excel. There are also other online applications, like www.trello.com, which has easy to use drag-and-drop features. Using mind-mapping applications like 'Simplemind' can really help when brainstorming for content ideas.

To get started you will simply need to map out and schedule the days of the week for each week of the year and decide what types of post you are going to create for certain days. You will need to balance the type of content in order to create variety and interest for your audience. You then need to create topics or themes and break the year down into weeks/months and make a schedule. You can add all the things that you are planning within your business, like offers, contests, product launches, and webinars, and then add all the things going on outside your business, like public holidays and special events. You need to incorporate all that information into your daily action plan.

It may seem daunting to look at a blank calendar, but you will be surprised how it comes together when you start breaking it down into months, weeks, and days. A posting calendar will help you keep your campaign focused, on track, and in line with your brand and your marketing goals and also keep it balanced in terms of the subject and type of media you use. A calendar will help you look ahead and help you to incorporate your marketing plan into your Twitter campaign. It may be that you are launching a new product, or maybe certain products tie in with specific holidays. You may have certain industry events you need to attend or are perhaps creating your own. Maybe you are going to run a competition at a certain time of the year. Whatever it is you are planning throughout the year, you need to include it on your calendar.

The following example shows how by creating a regular weekly schedule you can really simplify the process of creating your social media posting calendar:

Week 1
Monday
AM   Inspirational quote image to start the week.

PM   Post a useful tip.

Special Post Competition teaser.

Tuesday

AM   Link to weekly blog post with image.

PM   Caption this photo.

Wednesday

AM   Post a cartoon that relates to your niche.

PM   Post educational YouTube Video.

Thursday

AM   Post an engaging question which is business related (B2B)

PM   Post or share an infographic (B2B)

Special Post contest photo and entry details.

Friday

AM   Share a business tip (B2B)

PM   Post a weekend photo wishing all a happy weekend.

Special Holiday weekend post.

Saturday

AM   Post a question that is not business related.

Sunday

AM   Share a funny video.

PM   Post a relaxing image for a Sunday.

This is just an example and you obviously need to tailor make this to your business with the content that is important to your particular target audience.

CHAPTER THIRTEEN

PREPARING YOUR BUSINESS FOR SUCCESS

WHETHER YOUR SITE is being found through an organic search, an advertising campaign, Twitter, or any other social media platform, all your hard work is going to be wasted unless you have put a system in place to capture leads and convert them into customers. This system has to start from the moment your prospect either hits your website, your blog, or your Twitter profile, and your ultimate goal is to convert your browsers into buyers.

Firstly, the unfortunate fact is that the majority of your website visitors are unlikely to buy from you on their first visit. If you do not have a website that grabs their attention within the first couple of seconds, they will move very quickly onto another site. Secondly, even if your site does catch their eye, they are still likely to check out other sites and still may not return. To make any kind of impact at all your site needs to grab their attention and then capture their email address so you can continue your relationship with them through email. This chapter is going to take you through steps you will need to take, from getting your website or blog ready to setting up and creating your email campaign.

Email is still one of the most powerful ways to convert prospects into customers and has a conversion rate three times higher than social media conversion rates. That is not to say that your Twitter campaign is any less important, as this is where you are going to find and nurture your leads and transfer them to your opt-in by either capturing them on Twitter or on your website or blog. This chapter is going to take you through steps you will need to take from getting your website or blog ready to setting up and creating your email campaign.

PREPARING YOUR WEBSITE FOR SUCCESS

Whether you already have a website or blog or you are creating a new site from scratch, you need to make sure it has the necessary features to grab the attention of your target audience and capture their email addresses. Capturing the email addresses of your target audience has to be one of your most important goals when creating your website. Once your prospects have voluntarily submitted their email address, you have the opportunity to build a relationship, communicate your message, and promote your products and services on an ongoing and regular basis. A well thought-out and crafted email campaign can immediately establish trust and favor with your subscribers. Don't forget that it is you who owns your opt-in list and nobody can take it away from you. As long as you are providing your subscribers value with great content, they are likely to want to keep hearing from you. Remember you cannot rely on social media to continue your relationship as these platforms are changing all the time. You need to build your email list.

Once you have completed the exercise in the branding section and have your ideal customer persona or avatar, you will have a clear picture of what your target audience's pain point or problem is and how your product can help solve it or make their life better in some way. If you have a blog, and most businesses today need a blog, you will also have all the tools you need to create the right content to attract your target audience. Armed with this information you are halfway ready to putting a system in place, so your products sell themselves and your website is working like an extra sales person selling your products 24/7.

When your visitor arrives at your site, you have only three seconds to grab their attention. You need to connect emotionally with them and let them know immediately that they have arrived at the right place by communicating exactly how you are going to help them and what it is you are offering them.

Once they are on your site, you then need to win their interest and confidence so that they will voluntarily submit their email address. To do this you will need to create a lead magnet and offer your audience something which is incredibly valuable to them for free. There are numerous ways you can do this and which one you use will depend very much on what type of business you are and what your goals are. If you are a business offering technical solutions, you could offer them a free trial. If you are offering information, you could offer them a free report, a short video training series, or an ebook. If you are selling some kind of product or service, you could offer them a money-off voucher. These work particularly well for restaurants and the service industry as a whole. Whatever you are offering, it needs to be really good to attract your audience and get them to volunteer their email.

Here are the features you need to have on your website or blog or any landing page with a special offer.

- **Keep your design simple:** Your site needs to have a clean and simple design, and you need to communicate your most important message clearly and concisely to your target audience. Your most important content with any call-to-action needs to be placed above the fold, where they will be easily seen, and your call-to-action should have an easily seen button link rather than just a text link.
- **Make your site easy to navigate:** Really this is so important. Try to use the minimum number of pages you can and make your menu titles as easy to understand as possible.
- **Clearly communicate your message:** You want your visitors to subscribe to your opt-in, so you need to place your compelling offer with an image and title of the offer someplace where it is visible. The message and benefit of your offer needs be descriptive and specific.
- **Add a clear call-to-action:** In order for your visitors to sign up,

they will need to be told what to do. Make sure you have a direct call-to-action, for example, "Download your free ebook now" or "Sign up for your discount voucher now." Your call-to-action needs to be clearly visible with an eye-catching button link which is much more effective than a text link.

- **Add clear contact information:** Make it easy for your prospects to contact you by placing your contact details where they will be easily seen. With the technology available, you can even add chat features so that as soon as your prospect arrives on your site a chat form appears asking if you can be of any assistance. Obviously you need the resources to be able to man this, but it is an incredibly powerful way of quickly building trust and showing how much you value your website visitors by being available to answer any of their questions.

- **Email capture form:** Your email capture form needs to be as simple as possible, preferably just asking for their name and email. You need to state on the form that their email address is safe with you and will not be shared with anyone. Make sure your form is in a prominent position and consider using a pop-up form that appears 20 seconds after your prospect has arrived on your site. Your email sign-up form needs to go at the top, side, and bottom of your webpage and also on your 'about page,' which is often the most popular page on your site.

- **Privacy policy:** You need a clear privacy policy on your website to make it clear that you will not be spamming them or selling their information.

- **Thank you page:** Once your visitor has completed the form, you will have them as a lead, but before you let them go you can send them to a thank you page where you can offer them the opportunity to share your offer with their friends by including social sharing buttons.

- **Mobile Friendly:** You need to make sure your offer is easily visible and easy to complete on a cellphone. This is incredibly important, as more and more people are purchasing from their cellphone. There is nothing more annoying for the user than if the site is hard to navigate from their cellphone.

- Don't add external links to other sites. Be careful not to fall into the trap of wanting to make your site more interesting by adding lots of content and links to other external sites, as this will only detract from your main goals and you'll end up sending traffic away from your site.

Landing pages

Landing pages are incredibly effective if you want to promote specific offers for specific products to specific audiences. A landing page is a page that is designed to give information about an offer and then capture a lead with a form for your visitor to complete so that they can download or claim that offer. Landing pages are highly effective in capturing leads because they are designed to be specific in their goal, which is to capture the contact information of your visitor.

The landing page should have a clear, uncluttered design and not have any links or navigation menus that could take your visitor away from the landing page. It should contain the following:

- A headline (The title of the offer)
- A description of the offer, clearly detailing the benefits to your visitor
- A compelling image of the offer
- A clear call-to-action. This can be in the form of an image or text.
- A form to capture contact information (The fewer fields required to be completed, the more leads you will receive.)
- A clear privacy policy on your website that makes it clear that you will not be spamming them or selling their information
- A thank you page leading them to another offer or social sharing

You can either ask your web developer to create landing pages or there are numerous tools available on the Internet where you can easily create one, for example: www.leadpages.net, www.unbounce.com, www.launcheffect.com, and www.instapage.com

SETTING UP AND CREATING YOUR EMAIL CAMPAIGN

Once you have created your lead capture system on your website, blog, or separate landing page and have your subscribers' permission to send them your email, you are going to need a really good email campaign to convert those leads into sales.

Email is still one of the most effective forms of converting leads into sales, and email is more powerful than ever. Not only is it cost effective but it also provides one of the most direct and personal lines of communication with your customer. Once subscribed, they have invited you into their inbox on a regular basis and producing valuable content for your subscribers will develop trust and deepen your relationship with them. Your email will also work hand in hand with your Twitter campaign. As you build your relationship with your followers on Twitter , they are more likely to deem your emails valuable and open them.

The first thing you need to do is set yourself up with a good email marketing provider and there are many you can choose from: www.aweber.com, www.constantcontact.com, and www.mailchimp.com to name a few. It's important to use a system where you have a confirmed opt-in. This is when the subscriber is sent an email to confirm their email address. This verifies that you are gaining consent and legally protects you. It also helps you to keep a clean list, and it protects you from sending emails to incorrect addresses. You can then automate your emails with an auto responder and send out emails automatically over time.

Your next task is to plan and create your email campaign. Here are a few tips for doing so:

- **Be clear about your goals:** You need to be absolutely clear from day one what you want to achieve through email. Are you using it to introduce a new product at some time? Are you launching an event? Whatever you do, make sure you know exactly what it is that you want to achieve.

- **Keep it simple and in line with your branding:** Make sure your email design ties in with your branding. Most email providers offer templates which you can add your own branding to, or you can get a designer to create a particular design. Keep it really simple. Sometimes if things are too fancy they become impersonal.

- **Send a regular newsletter:** Plan to send a regular newsletter email at least once a month and once a week if you can. You can also plan to send off information about offers which tie in with special holidays and occasions throughout the year or competitions or events that you may be planning.

- **Plan your topics:** You need to plan the topics you want to cover in each email, and this should tie in nicely with the plan for your blog articles. You then need to deliver high quality content which is tailor-made to fit with your subscribers' interests, and it needs to be so good that they are looking forward to the next email from you. If you are sending emails about offers then you need to show them clearly how these offers are going to benefit their lives.

- **Attention-grabbing titles:** This is where you need to get really creative. Your main goal here is to get your subscriber to open your email, and you need to create a headline that is going to make your subscriber curious and inquisitive and eager to open your mail. Questions work really well as titles, and you will often see your open rates increase. This is because people find questions intriguing and they feel like you are directly addressing them. Try and avoid the words that will trigger spam filters. Simply search Google for a list of these words to avoid.

- **Be authentic and true to your brand:** Write your emails in a style that your audience will grow to recognize, 'like,' and identify with your brand. Write so your subscriber feels like you are just writing to them. You need to establish yourself as a likeable expert for your subscribers. Try and create a personal relationship with them by addressing them by name and giving them a warm friendly introduction. Offering them the opportunity to connect with you and answer any of their questions by simply replying to your mail is a great way to create a connection and trust.

- **Keep it simple** Make sure your emails are simply constructed and straight to the point so you keep your subscribers' interest and get them quickly to the place you want them to go, like your blog or offer.

- **Include social sharing buttons:** Include all your social sharing icons and links in your mail.

- **Make them feel safe:** Make sure your subscribers are clear that their email will not be shared and that they can unsubscribe anytime.

- **Analyze your open rates:** Most email service providers include statistics in their packages so you can analyze open rates, bounce rates, click through rates, unsubscribers, and social sharing statistics. These results give you the opportunity to find out what is and what is not working.

Chapter Fourteen

Blog Blog Blog

THIS CHAPTER IS for anyone who does not have a blog. The word blog has been mentioned numerous times throughout the book and has become an essential part of any online business today.

What is a Blog?

A blog (short for web log) is a term used to describe a website that provides an ongoing journal of individual news stories which are based around a certain subject or subjects (blog posts.) Blogs have given people the power of the media. Anyone can now create a personal type of news that appeals to a high number of small niche audiences.

Bloggers simply complete a simple online form with a title and body and then post it. The Blog post then appears at the top of the website as the most recent article. Over time the posts build up to become a collection of posts which are then archived chronologically for easy reference. Each blog post can then become a discussion with space for comments below the post, readers can leave comments and questions. This is where bloggers start to build relationships and a community with their readers and other bloggers who may have similar interests. Blogs were one of the earliest forms of social media and started growing in the late 1990s. The number of blogs has exploded in recent years and blogs now underpin the majority of successful social media campaigns.

Why Blog For Business?

Blogging is one of the most beneficial tools that a business has to communicate it's expertise and ideas to its prospects and customers and to engage with them. Businesses can share information about their business and about any subject that may be of interest to their niche. It is a fact that businesses with blogs benefit from an increase in the number of visitors to their website, increased leads, increase in inbound links and increased sales. Here are some of the reasons why and the benefits that come with blogging:

- **Underpins your whole social media campaign** Your blog is the focus of all your social media efforts and the centre of all your content marketing efforts. One of the main goals of any business today will be to get people to their blog to read their valuable and targeted content and social media will be one of the main tools they can use to drive traffic to their blog.

- **Increased website traffic** A well optimized blog will increase your chances of being found in search. Google loves unique fresh content and if this is created regularly, this will boost your traffic.

- Builds brand awareness A Blog offers a business the opportunity to build a community and build awareness for their products or services. The more people who see your blog, the more people see your brand.

- **Provides valuable information for your niche** Creating a Blog gives your business a voice and provides your niche with valuable information in relation to the subjects that they are interested in. This may include information about market trends, industry news and insight into your products and services and what is behind them.

- **Thought leadership** Sharing your expertise with valuable information will make you stand out as a thought leader in your particular field and will help you to build a professional online reputation.

- **Builds trust & creates warm leads** When you are providing valuable content for your niche on a regular basis, answering their questions and addressing their concerns, this in turn creates trust between you and your prospective customers. This trust leads to more leads and will result in sales. When your audience become regular readers of your blog they become warm rather than cold leads, the ice has been broken and they are half way there in terms of buying your product.

- **You gain more knowledge** While writing your blog you will be continually researching your subject, learning about new technology, products and new trends. In turn, this keeps you ahead of the game and in the eyes of your customers it makes you an expert. As time goes by you become more and more knowledgable and can steer your business in line with market trends and keep your products and services up to the minute. You will also find that blogging is inspiring and your ideas will snowball, as you learn more material you will find more material to blog about.

- **Interaction and feedback** When your blog has room for comments and discussion it will give you the opportunity to hear what people are saying, the questions they are asking and insight into what they want out of your products. Feedback like this is invaluable to your business and also leads to more ideas for more blog posts. This kind of feedback also encourages a conversation and you actually get the opportunity to communicate with prospective customers.

How to Create a Blog

Creating your blog is incredibly straight forward. There are a number of free blogging platforms that are available, however, if you read the terms and conditions of most of these platforms you will find that at the end of the day you do not actually own the content and you will not have full control of your blog. You will have no control of the advertising displayed, you are unlikely to be able to include an email capture form, you will not be able to have you own domain name and you will not be able to install plugins. With a free platform your domain name will look something like http://mybusinessblog.theirblogplatformname.com and overall it is not going to look that professional.

The best and safest way of creating a blog and running with your own domain name is to create one with wordpress.org or you can use website creators like www.wix.com or www.squarespace.com who both offer blogs with their product and you can add your own domain. Using any of these will give you full control over your site.

Wordpress.org is a free open source platform which means it can be modified and customized and by anyone. You can use custom themes or you can choose from hundreds of free themes and plugins. The wordpress.org blogging platform is free but you will need to purchase a domain name and host your site on your own server, however most hosting companies offer inexpensive monthly plans and a one click installation solutions. You will also need to make sure you back up your blog and you may very well find this is included in your hosting package.

WHAT MAKES A SUCCESSFUL BLOG?

For those businesses that are doing it right blogging can be hugely beneficial and they will often see an increase of over 50% of website visitors and leads. However, many blogs also fail to make any positive difference to a business, so it is essential that before you waste time and resources you understand what you need to do to create a successful blog:

Set Goals and objectives
First of all you will need to be about clear what your marketing goals are and set clear objectives for what you want to achieve from your blog.

Example Goal 1
Increase brand awareness through Twitter.
Objective:
Achieve X number of Retweets per month on Twitter.

Example Goal 2
Increase Traffic to website from blog.
Objective: To achieve an increase of X Traffic from blog.

Example Goal 3
Increase the number of leads for product A.
Objective: To gain X number of new opt-ins per week.

Example Goal 4
To create interaction and engagement.
Objective: To have at least X number of comments on each blog post.

Example Goal 5
To become a thought leader in the industry.
Objective: To write X number of guest posts per month/year.

Example Goal 6
To increase the ranking of blog in Google and Bing.
Objective: To achieve X number of backlinks from other websites in 6 months.

Create top content for your audience
Again it's all about your audience and what they want, what they are interested in, what makes them tick and what problems they need solving. If you can identify these things then you are half way to finding the valuable content that is going to keep your audience interested and engaged. When you create your content it needs to be either inspiring, educational, informative or entertaining. If you can create content that people really value, they are more likely to share your content, more likely to sign up for your updates and more likely to come back looking for more. Creating content around your product or services is not going to provide enough interest to your readers and it is unlikely to get shared. Of course the occasional post is ok but try and keep away from this unless you can tie it in with something which is of real value to your

audience.

Create a content plan

Your content plan is the backbone to your blog. You will need to decide what topics you are going to build your blog around so that you can stay consistent. There may be certain keywords that you want to target and need to incorporate into your content. Once you know your topics or subjects then you can decide which types of posts you are going to create. There are numerous types of blog posts you can use, for example; tutorials, how to's , interviews, reviews, book reviews, advice, Q and A's, case studies, trend reports and the latest news in your industry. When you have decided on all this you then write a schedule and if you have certain events that happen every year in your industry make sure you include these in your plan.

Newsworthy posts

Make sure you are blogging about whats new in your industry and keep an eye on trending topics relating to your industry so you can create blog posts that are really up to date. You can do this by checking out what is trending on the social sites and also signing up for Google alerts which will keep you up to date on new info relating to your interests and queries.

Frequent and consistent blogging

It is proven that the more high quality content you produce, the more views your blog will get. You will need to post at least once a week if not more. Google loves fresh content so the more posts you have, the more opportunities you are going to have to be found.

Optimize your blog for search

Look for keywords and phrases that people are looking for. There are tools available to do this like word tracker, Google trends and Google keyword planner. You can find out the amount of competition by typing a phrase into Google search and seeing how many results it brings up. In order to get found you will need to concentrate your efforts on low competition keywords and phrases and the more specific your words and phrases are the better. You can then create your content around your chosen keyword or phrase as long as the content is highly relevant. When creating your blog post make sure you put the word/phrase in the page title, the header and the body. If you put the phrase in your meta tag it will be displayed in bold font in the search results which will make it stand out even more.

Attention grabbing headline

To catch your readers attention you need a good headline, a headline that will need to intrigue your audience enough to make them feel that they absolutely have to read this post. It needs to be simple and to the point as well as containing valuable keywords. Here are some example headlines that really work:

How to ....

7 ways to successfully ....

Why you should do ..... to ....

Secrets that every ...... should know.

The secret formula for success in ......

5 quick and easy ways to ....

What every serious ...... should know about......

7 things every ..... should avoid to ......

A great design

Your blog needs to be inviting and although the content is what people are looking for the blog still needs to be visually appealing and reflect your brand. If your blog is just text based it's going to look cold and uninviting and lack interest, so you need to include compelling images to engage your audience. It is definitely a good idea to spend time researching different themes. Another thing to watch with your design is your side bar, make sure you have only what is absolutely necessary so you do not pull your readers attention away from the action you want them to take.

Formatting

You need to make it as easy as possible for your reader to read and digest your blog. If you format your blog with headings, bold subtitles and bullet points it will be a much more enjoyable to read than one long paragraph.

Ask a question at the end of your post

Asking a question at the end of your post is likely to provoke discussion. People like to think their opinions matter and it's a great way for your readers to interact and network with each other too. Make sure you answer any questions your readers ask, there is nothing worse than seeing bloggers ignoring their readers.

Tags

Tags help people to find your content within your blog and with the search engines, they also help to group related posts together.

11 THINGS EVERY BLOG SHOULD HAVE

An incentive to join your opt-in

One of the main goals of your blog is to captures leads. The majority of your readers will probably only read one of your blog posts so it's really important to try and get them on your opt-in list so they will keep reading your blog. You will need to make sure you give them some kind of incentive to complete the email capture form, like a free report, free ebook, or simply email updates.

An engaging image

A blog needs at least one image to make it look interesting and inviting. Blogs without images are simply boring. You can use your own images, stock photos, or images from photo sharing sites like Flickr.

Clear call-to-actions

You need to make it very clear both within and outside of your text. what you want your readers to do. This could be anything from signing up for email updates, a free trial, a free offer, a request for a quote, or more information on a product.

Email capture form

You can either include a prominent form on your blog or install a pop-up mail capture form. If you do install a pop-up then make sure the reader has a good few seconds to read the heading and start reading the article before the form pops up. It is also a good practice to put at least three email sign-up forms on the page, one below the article, one in the footer, and one on the top beside the article or right above it.

About section

Your "about" section is the introduction to you and your blog. It's probably the most viewed page of any blog. People like to know who is writing the blog and feel acquainted with that person, so you need to get your personality over in this section. Make sure you include your name and a picture of yourself. This will help your readers make a personal connection with you. A video of yourself is also a great a way of getting your readers acquainted too. Above all, focus on how you are going to help your readers, what problems you are going to solve for them, and introduce some of the topics you are going to talk about. Remember, your blog is about your audience's needs and not yours.

Contact page

A simple contact form works best but also make it really easy for people to reach out to you. Make sure you include all your social sharing buttons and an email capture form.

Easy to search archives

If the content of your blog posts is interesting your readers are going to want to read more so you need to make the previous blog posts easily accessible. On many sites it really is incredibly difficult to find content, so you need to get yourself a custom archive page. A search box at the top of your blog is a great idea for helping your readers find content.

Social sharing plug-ins

You need to include buttons or links to all the social networks where you have a presence. There are hundreds of plug-ins you can use to do this. Also make sure you have sharing buttons next to your articles as well.

RSS Feed

RSS (Rich Site Summary) is a format for delivering regularly changing content on the Internet. It saves you from checking the sites you are interested in for new content. Instead, it retrieves the content from sites you are interested in. Make sure you have the RSS feed and then have a clear call-to-action making it clear why they should subscribe to your feed. If you want to keep up-to-date with your favorite bloggers you can sign up to either My Yahoo, www.bloglines.com, or www.newsgator.com.

Comments section

Your blog needs a comment section which will encourage interaction and help you to build relationships with your readers. You can easily install Facebook comments with a WordPress plug-in. Disqus is another favorite comment provider.

A guest bloggers welcome page

Guest posting is becoming more and more important in the blogging community and making it obvious that you will accept guest posts is going to go a long way to building relationships with other bloggers. The benefits of having other people contributing to your blog are that you will have more valuable content on your site and more exposure if your guest blogger promotes their posts on their site. You may also gain from the opportunity to produce a guest post on their blog at a later date. Guest blogging is a top method of getting back links to your blog, which is essential for search engine optimization.

Privacy policy & terms of service pages

Make it clear your email readers are safe with you and you are not going to share their information with any other parties.

PROMOTING YOUR BLOG

If you want to run a successful blog, you cannot just rely on search to get it out into the blogosphere. You need to find other ways of promoting your content and getting found.

- **Promote on your social sites:** Posting your blog content on social sites is essential. You can connect your blog to Twitter and Facebook so your content is automatically shared. Or you can use Hootsuite or Tweetdec to share your content to multiple sites, which will save you time. When posting, use an image to grab your audience's attention and make sure you use popular hashtags for your topic which will open up more opportunities to being found by new people.

- **Guest blogging:** Guest blogging is a great way of gaining a larger following. It will also give your blog more exposure, credibility, and increase your inbound links, which is essential for SEO. Most bloggers allow guest bloggers to post their bio, including their social profiles and blog URL, on their site.

- **Social sharing buttons:** As mentioned previously, it is essential to have social sharing buttons next to your blog articles.

- **Comment on other blogs:** There is so much opportunity for you to promote yourself today with the number of blogs and social sites. If you comment on other peoples' blogs you can often leave a URL, but only if it is relevant to the article being commented on and you are adding some value to the article.

- **Website and email:** If you have a website then try and point people to your blog. You can do this by adding visual links on your "about" page and other pages. Also make sure you have a link to your blog in your email and send an email to your current contacts telling them about your blog.

- **Create a Google Adwords campaign:** If you are serious about driving traffic to your site and generating leads and you have your blog set up to catch leads and subscribers, an Adwords campaign may kick start your traffic while you are waiting for your blog to get found naturally in search results. Getting quick results like this will also allow you to see if your blog design and format is working and whether any incentives you are offering are enough to generate subscribers and leads.
- **Submit your blog to Reddit and Stumbleupon:** Both of these websites allow their users to rate web content. Reddit is a collection of webpages which have been submitted by its users. Stumbleupon is a collection of web pages that has been given the thumbs up. You can submit pages directly on its submit page or by installing the Firefox add-on or the Chrome extension. It is best not add too many of your own pages to Stumbleupon but make sure you add both the Reddit and Stumbleupon buttons to your blog so other people can.

THE ESSENTIAL WORDPRESS PLUGINS

One of the best things about WordPress for your blog is that it is easy to customize and you need little or no technical or design knowledge to create a great blog. There are a ton of plug-ins you can install to make your site even better, but there are so many it is difficult to choose which ones are really important. To help you, here are some plug-ins that are essential for your blog:

- **The Facebook comments plug-in:** Installing Facebook comments into your blog can be tricky, but with this easy to use plug-in you can easily administer and customize Facebook comments from your WordPress site. Another plug-in, **Facebook comments SEO,** will insert a Facebook comment form, Open Graph tags, and insert all Facebook comments into your WordPress database for better search engine optimization. When it comes to spammers, Facebook with Open Graph is managing to weed out spammers and trolls with great effectiveness. Facebook allows you to login with Facebook, Yahoo, and Microsoft Live.

- **Disqus comment system:** The other popular comment system Disqus replaces your WordPress comment system with comments hosted and powered by Disqus. It features threaded comments and replies, notifications and replies by email, aggregated comments and social mentions, full spam filtering, and black-and-white lists. Disqus allows you to login with Facebook, Twitter, and Google.

- **Facebook Chat:** This is great if you want to chat with your visitors in real time. When installed, Facebook Chat will display on the bottom right. This is great for supplying support on your site.

- **Broken Link Checker:** This essential plug-in scans your site and notifies you if it finds any broken links or missing images and then lets you replace the link with one that works.

- **RB Internal Links:** This plug-in assists you with internal links and cuts the risk of error pages and broken links.

- **Social Sharing Plugins:** There are numerous social sharing plugins available for WordPress. **Flare** is a simple yet eye-catching sharing bar that you can customize depending on which buttons you want to display. It helps to get you followed or 'liked' and helps get your content shared via posts, pages, and media types. The other great feature Flare has is that you can display your Flare at the top, bottom, or right of your post content. When Flare is displayed on the left and right of your posts, it follows your visitors down the page and conveniently hides when not needed. Other social sharing plug-ins include: **Floating Social Media Icon, Social Stickers,** and **Shareaholic,** to name but a few.

- **All-In-One Schema Rich Snippets:** Rich snippets are markup tags that webmasters can put in their sites in order to tell Google what type of content they have on their site so that Google can better display it in search results. It is basically a short summary of your page. Rich snippets are very interactive, let you stand out from your competition, and help with your search engine ranking. Unless you are a techie then implementing them can be tricky. However, this plug-in makes it really simple by giving you a meta box to fill in every time you create a new blog post.

- **Contact Form Plug-ins:** It is very important to make it easy for your visitors to contact you, and a form really does help with this. There are numerous plug-ins available for you to easily install, and here are a few: **Contact 7, Fast Secure Contact form, Contact form, and Contactme.**

- **Simple Pull Quote:** The Simple Pull Quote WordPpress plug-in provides an easy way for you to insert and pull quotes into your blog posts. This is great for bringing attention to important pieces of information and adding interest to a post.

- **Backup Plug-ins:** Backing up your files and database is essential. It may be that your hosting service provides this, but there are very good plug-ins that do this: Vaultpress, BackWPup, Backup buddy, and Backup.

- **Related Posts Plug-ins:** Related post plug-ins help your visitors to stay on your site by analyzing the content on your site and pulling in similar articles from your site for them to read. One of the most popular ones is **nrelate related** content which is simple to install and activate. **WordPress related posts** is another one.

- **Search Everything Plug-in:** This plug-in increases the ability of the WordPress search, and you can configure it to search for anything you choose.

- **Google Analytics Plugin:** The Google Analytics plug-in allows you to easily integrate Google Analytics using Google Analytics tracking code.

- **Google XML Sitemaps:** It is essential that the search engines can index your site and this plug-in will generate a special XML sitemap.

- **SEO Friendly images:** This plug-in automatically adds alt and title attributes to all your images, which helps to improve traffic from search engines.
- **Akismet (Comments and Spam):** The more traffic you receive, the more likely it is for you to receive spam and fake comments. Akismet checks your comments against Akismet web services to see if they look like spam or not and then lets you review it under your comments admin screen.
- **Social Author Bio:** Social Author Bio automatically adds an author box along with Gravatar and social icons on posts.
- **Thank Me Later:** This great little plug-in automatically sends a thank you note by email to anyone who has commented on your blog. You can personalize your email and set up exactly when you want to send it, and you can set it up to only send it out once or as a chain of emails. This plug-in is great for engaging people who comment on your blog, and you could use it to encourage people to join your opt-in.

MEASURING YOUR RESULTS

Measuring the success of your blog is crucial in order to steer your blog in the right direction so that your business can benefit from all the rewards a top blog can offer. Here are a number of ways you can measure your success:

Google Analytics

You can easily measure the number of social media shares, number of leads, subscribers, and comments on your blog. For more detailed information on your blog performance, setting up a Google Analytics account is essential and will offer you a wealth of detailed information so you can measure results, including the following:

- **The number of back links:** In the left side bar under **Standard Reports** you will find a section **Traffic Sources,** and then under

Social, you will find **Trackbacks**. You will find here any web pages that have linked to any page of your site with the number of visits.

- **The number of visits:** Obviously this is one of the most important statistics, and you will be able to easily see how many visits you have and information about where your traffic is coming from.

- **Page views:** You will be able to see which pages are generating the most interest, and therefore, you will be able to plan more content similar to this.

- **Keywords:** You can keep track of your success with how your traffic is being generated by keywords. You will be able to see if your optimization for certain keywords are working and whether your blog is being found by keywords that you had not considered. When you identify which keywords are the most popular, you can try and work them into other blog posts.

- **Conversions:** In Google Analytics you will also be able to track conversions, which is an action on your site that is important to your business. This could be a download, sign up, or purchase. You will need to define your goals in analytics in order to track the conversion. You will be able to see conversion rates and also the value of conversions if you set a monetary value. There are detailed instructions available in Google Analytics on how to set this up, or you can employ a web developer or specialist to do it.

Chapter Fifteen

The Icing on the Cake

FOLLOWING ALL THE steps, instructions, and strategies is going to go a long way to making your campaign succeed, but what does it take to make you really good? If you have ever followed or are following certain brands on social media, you will probably have discovered that there are certain brands or businesses that stand out from the crowd. These are the brands and businesses that seem bigger than their products. These are the ones who usually have a sizeable and highly targeted audience, the best quality content, the greatest amount of interaction and engagement, and often post viral content. They literally have their audience hanging on their every word and get the highest open rates for their emails. They appear to understand their audience and relate to them by going out of their way by either helping them to achieve their dreams, calm their fears or confirm their suspicions, and offer them incredible value. It is obvious by the interaction that they have built a loving and respecting community, and you can be almost sure that all this is transferring to their balance sheets. These businesses are what I call 'The Social Media Superstars.' They are the game changers and they truly know how to leverage the power of social media to work for their business.

These 'Social Media Superstars' can often be compared to those party animals who always seem to be the most popular at any party and are more often than not surrounded by an audience of engaged and happy people having a great time. These people also always seem to be the most interesting, the most interested, the most charismatic, and the most engaged. They almost always tend to be good listeners as well. So how can you emulate this scenario, and what does it take to stand out from the crowd in Twitter marketing?

It's all about your audience and a few other things!

The reasons these individuals, businesses, and brands are good at social media marketing is not because they have particular powers. It's not by chance or coincidence. It's because they know that it's all about the audience and a few other things!

Of course your aim is to ultimately benefit your business, but in order to do this you need to make it all about your audience and what they want. If you give them what they want by either making their life better or easier in some way or solving a problem they may have, then you are going to build a valuable base of fans who trust you, open your emails, and are ready to go to the next step and buy your product. You will find that your fans will become ambassadors and advocates and will then be doing the work for you by sharing your content and promoting your brand in the most powerful way, word-of-mouth. To achieve this and stand out from the crowd, you need to go the extra mile by doing the following:

- Being fully committed and positive about your campaign and in it for the long term
- Totally believing in what you are offering. This could be your product, your service, or yourself, if you are a personal brand.
- Making it all about your audience, knowing exactly who they are, what makes them tick, what they need, and how to connect with them
- Putting your audience's needs above your own and demonstrating the rich content and service you provide
- Putting the relationship with your audience first, by listening to them, understanding them, and embracing conversation where you can
- Offering your audience incredible value with free information and advice
- Being authentic and true to your brand

So if there is one piece of insight I want to leave you with, it is this:

IT'S ALL ABOUT YOUR AUDIENCE and WHAT THEY WANT

I really hope you have enjoyed the book, have found it of great value, and that you will continue using it as your manual for your success on Twitter. The world of social media is continually changing, and it is my commitment to keep updating the books when these changes happen. If you would like to continue receiving these social media updates by email, please sign up at www.alexstearn.com

I would love your feedback about the book and would be very grateful if you could take just a moment to leave a review on Amazon at this link . By leaving a review you can also enter the Prize draw for a Kindle Fire HD at this link and of course please feel free to contact me if you have any questions at alex@alexstearn.com

I have also written a series covering all the major social media platforms including: Facebook, Google + , Pinterest, Instagram, Tumblr, YouTube and the Big Book ,Make Make Social Media Work for your Business which includes all the books, available on Amazon from $9.99 available at this link http://bit.ly/alexauthor

Lastly, I have also set up a group on Facebook called 'Make Social Media Work for your Business.' The group was created for supporting each other in our social media efforts, for networking, and also as a place for finding out about the latest social media developments. You can join at this link http://bit.ly/yourgroup

Website: www.alexstearn.com

www.twitter.com/alexstearncom
www.facebook.com/alexandrastearn
www.instagram.com/alexstearn

Make Twitter Work For Your Business

www.twitter.com/alexstearncom
www.pinterest.com/alexstearn
www.alexstearn.tumblr.com
www.youtube.com/alexstearn
www.google.com/+alexstearn
www.linkedin.com/in/alexstearn

Other Books in the Series

<u>Make Social Media Work for your Business</u>

The complete series in one book!

The complete guide to marketing your business, generating new leads, finding new customers and building your brand on Twitter, LinkedIn, Pinterest, Instagram Google +, Tumblr, YouTube, Facebook, Foursquare, Vine and Snapchat.

<u>Make Facebook Work for your Business</u>

<u>Make Instagram Work for your Business</u>

<u>Make Pinterest Work for your Business</u>

<u>Make Google + Work for your Business</u>

<u>Make YouTube Work for your Business</u>

<u>Make Tumblr Work for your Business</u>

We'd love to hear from you

Thank you for your recent purchase of 'Make Twitter Work for your Business' I really hope you have enjoyed the book and your business will benefit greatly.

If you have any questions about the book or about social media marketing in general, please do not hesitate to contact me by email at **alex@alexstearn.com** or contact me Twitter or Facebook and I will do my best to reply as soon as possible. I also offer regular updates, ebooks and social media tips in my newsletter at www.alexstearn.com and a group on Facebook which is all about supporting each other in our social media efforts and networking. Would love you to join us at this link http://bit.ly/yourgroup

Lastly, if you have enjoyed the book I would be so grateful if you could leave a review on Amazon, your feedback is so valuable and also helps others benefit from your experience.

Looking forward to seeing you in the group ッ

17657837R00096

Printed in Poland
by Amazon Fulfillment
Poland Sp. z o.o., Wrocław